TRUE FAITH IN

THE TRUE GOD

AN INTRODUCTION TO LUTHER'S

LIFE AND THOUGHT

TRUE FAITH IN THE TRUE GOD

AN INTRODUCTION TO LUTHER'S

LIFE AND THOUGHT

HANS SCHWARZ

TRANSLATED BY MARK WILLIAM WORTHING

Augsburg

MINNEAPOLIS

TRUE FAITH IN THE TRUE GOD
An Introduction to Luther's Life and Thought

Scripture quotations from the New Revised Standard Version Bible, copyright © 1989 by the Division of Christian Education of the National Council of the Churches of Christ in the U.S.A.

The cover illustration, courtesy of the Religious News Service, shows Martin Luther nailing the Ninety-five Theses to the door of the castle church in Wittenberg on October 31, 1517, which is generally considered the beginning of the Reformation.

Cover design by Craig P. Claeys
Text design by David Meyer

Library of Congress Cataloging-in-Publication Data

Schwarz, Hans, 1939–
    True faith in the true God: an introduction to Luther's life and thought / by Hans Schwarz.
       p. cm.
    Includes bibliographical references.
    ISBN 0-8066-2821-9 (alk. paper)
    1. Luther, Martin, 1483-1546. 2. Reformation—Biography.
I. Title.
BR325.S3335 1996
284. 1 092—dc20
[B]

96-4127
CIP

The paper used in this publication meets the minimum requirements of American National Standards for Information Sciences—Permanence of Paper for Printed Library Materials, ANSI Z329.48-1984.   ∞

Manufactured in the U.S.A.   AF 9-2821

3   4   5   6   7   8   9   10

CONTENTS

PREFACE

The life of the great reformer Martin Luther remains fascinating to this day, and there is no shortage of accounts and assessments of his life. But the situation is different with his teaching. Although there are more than 100 volumes of Luther's writings in the authoritative German Weimar edition, it is difficult to give an account of Luther's teaching. It is therefore not surprising than even experts in the field of Luther research scarcely dare to sketch a comprehensive presentation of Luther's thought. The most recent efforts available in English by the Erlangen Luther scholar Paul Althaus are already 30 years old (*The Theology of Martin Luther* [1962], Philadelphia: Fortress, 1966; and *The Ethics of Martin Luther* [1965], Philadelphia: Fortress, 1972).

This book is not an attempt to replace or correct the life work of Paul Althaus and other Luther scholars. Its purpose rather is to give an overview of Luther's life and thought. The first chapter of this book is a brief biographical overview of the most important phases in Luther's life. Chapters 2 through 11 lead directly to the center of Luther's teachings and are illustrated with quotations from Luther's own writings to provide insight into his way of thinking. When one understands the concerns that lay on Luther's heart, connecting lines can easily be drawn to other areas of Luther's thought that are not considered in this book. To cover the entire theology and ethics of Martin Luther, many more areas would need to be considered. Yet the concern here is with the center of Luther's theology. Understanding this core of thought will allow us to appreciate Luther, as well as his primary concerns with a living and productive faith in God.

At this point, I would like to express my heartfelt thanks to Dr. Jens Colditz for his valuable assistance in the completion of this manuscript. He not only assisted with stylistic improvements in the text but also frequently offered good criticisms regarding the content of the manuscript itself. Hildegard Ferme deserves thanks for the careful production of the manuscript and for her alert assistance through the various stages of its evolution. Dr. Mark Worthing, my former graduate research assistant, voluntarily took upon himself the task of translating this book from the original German. My best thanks to him for his fine cooperation and help in rendering this text into English.

HANS SCHWARZ

INTRODUCTION

Martin Luther altered the face of Western Christianity more than anyone either before or after him. The reaction to his work led to a split in the West between the "tradition" believers and the adherents of the Reformation. Yet it would be a distortion of the facts to charge Luther with the greatest church schism of all time, because the exclusion of the reformers from the church was instigated by the Romans. In addition, the framework of Western Christianity had been experiencing tremors for some time before Luther. Since the work of John Wycliffe (ca. 1320-1384) in England and John Huss (ca. 1368-1415) in Bohemia (present-day Czech Republic), frequent criticism had been voiced against the centralizing efforts of Rome. In the century of the Reformation, the struggle to regionalize the church reached new heights. Yet a regional church had always been presupposed in Eastern Christendom. One could nevertheless accuse Luther of destroying the doctrinal unity of the church. But even this unity between East and West had been irreparably destroyed through the edict of the Roman Pope Leo IX against the Eastern church on July 16, 1054, which formalized the separate doctrinal development of the Western church. One could even credit Luther with encouraging a return to the doctrinal tradition of the early church and for rejecting the separate dogmatic and theological development of the West, at least to the extent that, according to his understanding, this development contradicted fundamental biblical teaching.

Much more important than this, however, is the positive influence Luther exerted. On one hand he noticed the similarity of his teaching with that of John Huss, while on the other hand he exchanged position statements with King Henry VIII, who aspired to create in England a church that was independent from Rome. Also not to be overlooked is Luther's considerable influence on the Reformed wing of the Reformation led in Switzerland by both Huldreich Zwingli and John Calvin. Both of these reformers made great effort (as can be seen, for instance, in their debates with Luther over the Lord's Supper) to come as close as possible to his teaching. Even the left wing of the Reformation, from Kaspar Schwenkfeld to Balthasar Hubmaier, was touched by Luther's ideas. Decisive for the Reformation in the West was also the fact that those loyal to the Roman church, as was demonstrated at the Council of Trent (1545-1563), eliminated unnecessary ballast and returned to the center of the Christian faith even while rejecting what they held to be ideals of the Reformation. It was no accident, therefore, that the Council of Trent devoted ample time to the doctrine of justification. Without the influence of the ideas of Luther, such an emphasis would have been impossible.

Luther is of such central importance for Western Christianity that it is always helpful to recall the crucial data of his life and the core of his teaching. Of course 500 years separate us from Martin Luther, during which time the world and intellectual history have decisively changed. It is sometimes claimed that Luther stood at the beginning of the modern period. In this regard, how-ever, one cannot overlook the fact that Luther lived before the Enlightenment and would have viewed our modern industrial society with wonder, if not as something entirely incomprehensible. "How do I find a gracious God?"—the central question of Luther's life that led him first into the monastery and pressed him next toward reformation—sounds strangely outdated today. In Luther's day, however, it was a pressing question, since the shorter life expectancy made it questionable whether one would even life to adulthood. Luther had experi-enced this painfully in his own family. Two of Luther's six children, born to his wife Katharina von Bora, died before they reached adulthood. Luther himself was blessed with a long life. Nevertheless, he was an ill and frail man by the time he died at age sixty-two. His body was weary and had been scarred from vari-ous ailments. It is no wonder, then, that for people of that period the earth offered little and they hoped at least for a better afterlife. Yet for this they need-ed first of all a gracious God, who would not reject them but instead would receive them into a better afterlife once their sojourn in this earthly valley of tears had ended.

When Luther inquired about a gracious God, he expressed a yearning shared by nearly all of his contemporaries. In a medieval family of seven chil-dren, one or two were expected to reach adulthood and have descendants of their own. In our small modern families, however, if even one child is severed from this life through an auto accident, no one remains to carry on the tradi-tion to the next generation. Yet what does "our tradition" mean when our communal character is so meager than many do not marry, or soon abandon their spouses? Stability and continuity are not characteristics of our modern society. Although we often believe that have most things under control, we are haunted by fear: the fear of meaninglessness, the fear of losing our jobs, the fear of finishing life empty-handed. Our effort to immediately satisfy every desire, to celebrate today rather than tomorrow, and still to gain some satisfaction out of life points to the fact that we are driven by anxiety.

The Reformation discovery of Luther can still have a liberating effect on us today. We need not be anxious, for we are not limited to our own selves and our own accomplishments. God is in charge, the God who has always been gra-cious and concerned for us. Luther disliked theological speculations, because he was convinced that they led to doubt and uncertainty. But he also strongly rejected looking first to humans and their potential, and then to God as a metaphysical scapegoat. In Luther's thought, God occupied first place. Only when God is on our side, the God from whom and to whom we have our being and without whom we cannot accomplish anything, can we meet the future with confidence. The endeavor to accord the divinity of God first place runs through Luther's entire thought. Already in the battle hymn of the Reformation Luther stresses, "No strength of ours can match his might! We would be lost, rejected." Luther was more than a seeker after God. He discovered in an existentially decisive matter that the God who created the whole universe is not an indifferent cosmic snob nor a fatalistically threatening judge, but instead a God who desires only the best for us and opens for us a new and certain future. Luther arrived at this knowledge because he saw the human face of God in Jesus Christ. In Jesus he recognized the gracious God. Through Jesus, Luther became aware that faith did not mean assent to ecclesiastically derived propositions but rather trust and reliance on the God who leads us to new shores.

1

LIFE AND WORK

Martin Luther, in all likelihood, was born on November 10, 1483. Efforts were later made to date his birth to the year 1484, because it was believed that a conjunction of planets in that year pointed to the beginning of an important new religious development. Hence Luther's colleague Philip Melanchthon, in contrast to Luther himself, sought to date Luther's birth to 1484. What is certain, however, is that Luther was born in Eisleben, a small village on the eastern edge of the Harz forest. It is also certain that the day after his birth he was baptized in the parish church of St. Peter and Paul and given the name of the patron saint of that day, Martin of Tours. He remained only a few months in Eisleben, where his family had moved from the village of Möhra, before they finally settled in nearby Mansfeld.

LUTHER'S EARLY LIFE AND EDUCATION

Luther always stressed that he had humble origins: "I am the son of peasants. My great-grandfather, grandfather, and father were all simple farmers."[1] Actually, his father, Hans Luder, worked his way up from simple miner in the Mansfeld copper mine to overseer. Hans eventually became co-owner of a copper mine and, after some years, of several more mines. In 1491 he was numbered among the four lords of Mansfeld who represented the citizens and worked with the city council. In contrast to his ancestors, therefore, he had achieved a considerable level of success. Hence when Martin Luther said of his parents in 1533, "In his youth my father was a poor miner. My mother carried all her wood on her back. It was in this way that they brought us up," one should not conclude that Luther grew up in poverty.[2] His parents were naturally very frugal. Only in this way were they able to achieve a certain measure of prosperity.

Their upbringing of their children was strict. For Hans it was clear that a son should achieve an even higher standard of living than the parents. And to achieve this Martin needed a good education. Therefore, between 1491 and 1501 Luther attended consecutively the Latin schools in Mansfeld, Magdeburg, and Eisenach. He had no good memories of the school in Mansfeld, which he compared to a "prison" and "hell." Luther received many whippings there, and he learned very little.[3] The school in Magdeburg, on the other hand, appears not to have been as bad. Students there learned the Latin of the medieval period and Christian hymns. If the students were caught speaking German while school was in session, they were beaten. Shortly before Easter 1497, Luther's father decided to send his son along with a friend to a school in Magdeburg that enjoyed a good reputation, managed by the Brothers of the Common Life. But this school too did not particularly impress Luther.

After only a year Martin was brought back to Mansfeld, and from there was sent to Eisenach, where several relatives of the family lived. Martin was enrolled there in the community school of St. George. He also sang in the boys' choir and gathered contributions for it from the residents of the town, as did the other boys. It was through this activity that he came into contact with the Schalbe family and their active religious life. This family had given significant bequests to the small Franciscan monastery at the foot of the castle at Wartburg. Luther thus had the opportunity to eat regularly with the family. Another significant influence on Luther during this period was the vicar at St. Mary's, Johannes Braun, who was to become a fatherly friend to him long beyond his stay in Eisenach. Also in this connection was the Cotta family, who were related to the Schalbes. Both families were well off and were represented in the city council. Through the Cotta family Luther learned to appreciate good music and was exposed to a good family life, which he still spoke of years later. The years he spent in Eisenach were the happiest of his youth and in 1530 he still referred to Eisenach as his "dear city."[4] It was here that the trembling youth was transformed into a happy young man. After three years there, at age eighteen it was time for him to begin university studies. Only two cities came into question: Leipzig, which was geographically closer, and Erfurt, which was more progressive. Luther's father decided on Erfurt, since he didn't want to save money by sending his son to the wrong place.

Erfurt was at the time one of the three or four largest cities in Germany. It lay at the intersection of major transportation routes and its economy was booming. In 1483 the cathedral in Erfurt received a new organ, which was one of the most famous in Germany, comparable to that of St. Peter's Cathedral in Rome. Twelve different religious orders influenced the life of the church in Erfurt, where there was a great veneration of relics. Erfurt therefore proudly called itself "the little Rome." Nuremburg was at that time only half the size of Erfurt, which with more than 10,000 residents was the largest city in which Luther ever lived.

In the summer semester of 1501, Luther began his studies at the University of Erfurt to complete the standard foundational studies in the arts. The program consisted of the so-called *trivium* of grammar, dialectic, and rhetoric, required for the bachelor's degree; and the *quadrivium* of arithmetic, astronomy, geometry, and music, required for the master of arts degree. The core of the trivium was dialectic, that is, logic, while the quadrivium was dedicated mostly to mathematics. This study typically lasted four years and was characterized by rigorous memorization and recitation.

Luther lived in a student dormitory that enjoyed a good reputation despite the fact that it was commonly known as the *Biertasche* ("beer bag"). Residents were required to rise at 4:00 A.M. and to be in bed by 8:00 P.M. The clothing was uniform and the meals were prescribed. Within the academic program itself, one had to complete a certain plan of studies, at the end of which the master's examination was taken. Even regular attendance at worship services was required. Nevertheless, Luther managed to enjoy himself along with the other students and did not neglect his social life. One of his fellow students, humanist Crotus Rubeanus, later said of Luther, "You were at once the musician and learned philosopher of our company."[5] Luther, however, did not waste his time and completed the trivium with his bachelor's examinations in the autumn of 1502. Afterward he devoted himself to the scientific, metaphysical, and ethical writings of Aristotle and studied the disciplines of the quadrivium. On January 7, 1505, the earliest possible date, he took the master's examinations and was second best of seventeen successful candidates. Luther later recalled with pleasure the graduation festivities with all the accompanying academic ceremonies. Luther's father was, of course, greatly pleased with the good performance of his son and addressed him thereafter with the respectful and formal *Ihr*, rather than the informal German *Du*. Although Luther later distanced himself somewhat from the value of a university education, he continued to take pleasure in the Latin classics.

After earning his master's degree, Luther was required to teach for two years in the faculty of arts. He was also allowed to use this time to study in one of the three higher faculties of medicine, theology, or law. Erfurt was not at all known for medicine and theology did not fit into the plans of Luther's father. Hence only law remained—an option that also held the promise of a successful career. Luther's father even had bought Martin's legal books for him and had already found a potential bride from an affluent family for his son. Thus Luther began attending lectures on April 24, 1505, and began his study of law on May 20. A month later he returned to Mansfeld and remained there with his parents for a week.

During the return journey on July 2, a few hours outside Erfurt near the small town of Stotternheim, Luther was surprised by a very severe thunderstorm. A bolt of lightning struck down very near him, and the jolt threw him to the ground. In fear of death he cried out, "Help me, Saint Anne! I will become a monk!"[6] For Luther the study of law was over. Luther was very familiar with St. Anne, the "grandmother" of Jesus, who was one of the most venerated saints of the late Middle Ages and the patron saint of miners. Just why Luther made good on his vow we may never precisely understand. We have only hints: that from the very beginning he was never particularly enthusiastic about the study of law, that he was very shaken by the sudden death of a close friend in 1505, and that he had already had positive experiences with the theological writings of Thomas Aquinas (1225–1274) and William of Occam (ca. 1285–1349). The theory that the psychological confrontation with his father played a role is likely unfounded, since that conflict arose in earnest only after Luther's decision to become a monk. Luther, speaking in 1539, said,

> Afterward I regretted having made the vow and many tried to dissuade me from it. I remained by my vow, however, and invited many good friends on the day of Alexius [July 16] to a farewell party since on the next day they would bring me to the monastery. As they sought to prevent me, however, I said, "Today you see me but never again!" Then they accompanied me with tears in their eyes. My father was very angry because of the vow but I remained firm in my decision and never considered leaving the monastery.[7]

A great conflict arose between Martin Luther and his father, who had an entirely different life in mind for his son. He also wrote him an angry letter in which he once again addressed him with the informal *Du*. In some ways Hans was more modern in his thinking than his son. He was the modern, success-oriented person for whom the family's climb in society was more important than the greatest religious sacrifice one could bring to God. Although he gladly welcomed priests and members of religious orders into his home, he did not feel obligated to them. When a priest once sought to convince him to give a special donation to the church, he answered, "I have many children. I will leave it to them since they need it more."[8] Martin, on the other hand, saw the religious life as a goal worthy of striving for, even though monasticism had already lost much of its former prestige and had become increasingly the object of disdain and ridicule.

Martin Luther went against the warnings of his friends and father, and entered the monastery. In Erfurt alone he had the choice between six different monasteries. From among these Luther decided to enter the monastery of the Augustinian Eremites. The monastery of this order of mendicants operated a theological school and belonged to the reform-minded branch of the Augustinian Eremites. The rules of the monastic life were taken especially seriously and were strictly observed. Of all his books, Luther took only the works of the Latin poets Plautus and Virgil with him into the monastery.

After about six weeks, Luther began his novitiate. He was assigned a cell, clothed in the monastic garb, had his head tonsured so that only a small circle of hair remained, and had to apply himself to physical labor. This included not only cleaning the monastery but also begging for donations from the residents of the city in the customary way of that time. The life of the Augustinian Eremite was strictly regulated. Luther, for instance, had to walk with his head bowed and his eyes directed toward the ground, and he was allowed something to drink only during meal times. Of course, he was also given a Latin Bible, the text of which he soon learned so well that he could immediately find any reference.

Luther fulfilled the requirements of his novitiate to the full satisfaction of his superiors. After the first year it was unanimously decided that he be allowed to make religion his profession. Shortly thereafter, Luther was informed that he was to become a priest. In preparation for this position, he had to learn the detailed explanations of the canon of the Mass by the Tübingen theology professor Gabriel Biel (1410–1495). Biel, the last important representative of Occamism, influenced him greatly. On April 4, 1507, Luther was consecrated a priest in the cathedral of Erfurt. On May 2 he celebrated his first mass in the monastery church, to which he invited his father at the instigation of his superiors. Surprisingly, his father accepted the invitation and appeared in Erfurt in the company of twenty friends on horseback, most likely with the intention of impressing the monks. At the reception following the Mass, a conversation took place between he and his father that revealed that Hans still disagreed with his son's decision. He reminded Martin of the honor a son owes his parents and argued in regard to the "appearance" at Stotternheim: "Just so it wasn't a phantom you saw!"[9]

Martin Luther, however, remained firm in his commitment. He next studied the general curriculum of his order and then theology at the University of Erfurt. In the autumn of 1508 he was suddenly sent to Wittenberg to teach moral philosophy on the faculty of arts there. The University of Wittenberg was founded in 1502 by the elector Frederick the Wise. The town itself, as Luther commented in 1532, lay on the edge of civilization. Luther was not especially happy about his new assignment. In autumn of the following year, Luther was back in Erfurt and had completed his theological studies, earning the rank of *Sentenciar*, which meant that he was now qualified to interpret the Sentences of Peter Lombard (ca. 1100–1160). Before he could hold his first lecture, however, he was called back to Wittenberg. It was in Wittenberg that he lectured on the *Sentences* until 1510.

In the meantime, a conflict had developed within his order between the rigorists and those advocating a more conventional practice. On account of this conflict, the superior of the German rigorist Augustinian community, Johann von Staupitz, sent Luther together with an Augustinian monk from Nuremburg to Rome to have the problem settled there. This was the greatest journey that

Luther would ever undertake, and the only one that would take him into a foreign country. The journey left a great impression upon him. Luther did not see Rome through the eyes of a tourist but came with the intention of taking full advantage of the city's treasure of relics. It was only later that the worldliness of the priests and the opulence of the cardinals' palaces left a negative impression on him. In 1510, however, he was very much impressed by the treasures of relics and the many holy sites. He took his assignment seriously and celebrated the Mass in all the important churches of the city.

Shortly after his return from Rome, Luther was transferred to Wittenberg once again, probably in September 1511. Johann von Staupitz had so much to do involving the administration of the Augustinian order that he needed to give up his position as professor of biblical interpretation. So that the order would not lose this position, Luther's studies leading to a doctor of theology were accelerated and his promotion took place in October 1512. In his doctoral oath Luther not only committed himself to obedience to the church but also to theological truth, a commitment he often referred to in the following years. Frederick the Wise was so interested in seeing his new university expand that he paid the required academic fees of the theologian of the mendicant order for his doctoral degree.

FROM PROFESSOR TO REFORMER

After the completion of his doctorate, Luther became a professor of biblical exegesis on the theological faculty of the University of Wittenberg, a position that he held until his death. Despite his academic career, Luther found no rest in his spiritual life. He sensed the wrath of God more keenly than most others of his time. Even the study of the Bible did not help him, because there he read only of the righteousness of God. How could he hope to stand up before divine righteousness? The church answered that this was done by obtaining the grace of God through the sacraments. But the most important sacrament, Holy Communion, was of no help to him here, since the preconditions of its worthy reception were humility and repentance. Luther was never certain whether he was repentant enough and whether he had confessed everything he should, regardless of how frequently he confessed. Hence he was unable to experience the peace that the sacraments were supposed to bring. Even good works were of no help to him. He recognized clearly the egoism that was concealed within the performance of good works. One did not perform such works freely or out of gratitude toward God but rather to win God's favor. Even the figure of Christ brought no peace to him, because he had learned to know Christ as judge, not as savior.

Luther, however, was not left alone in his doubt and spiritual turmoil. Johann von Staupitz, the head of Luther's order and the person who had pushed for Luther to work toward a doctoral degree and to succeed him as professor of biblical exegesis in Wittenberg, took Luther under his wing. Staupitz saw something useful in Luther's struggles, for without these Luther would probably have become a proud and perhaps even arrogant academician. As Luther continually brought the problem of his sinfulness before his confessor, however, Staupitz admonished him that he had never committed any "real" sins and that he should not bother Christ with trivia. He also helped him positively with his problems by explaining that genuine repentance begins with the love of righteousness and of God, and that what scholastic theology views as the last stage of repentance, namely God's love, is really its beginning. Repentance does not lead to a righteous and loving God; rather it proceeds from this God. Similarly, Staupitz sought to explain to Luther how he should think of the question of predestination. One must begin by contemplating the wounds of Christ, inflicted on him for our sake, and not with the question of whether one has been elected or rejected. With this starting point, the debate about predestination can be positively settled. In 1520 Staupitz gave up his office as general superior of the Augustinian order and went to Salzburg to become the abbot of the Benedictine monastery of St. Peter. In later years Luther continued to express his gratefulness to Staupitz, but also regretted that this man who had been so influential on him remained with his pre-Reformation faith and labeled Luther's followers as heretics.

The decisive breakthrough that led to Luther's Reformation-oriented thought came in the so-called tower experience in which it became clear to Luther through his reading of Romans 1:17 that the righteousness of God is not that righteousness with which God judges us but the righteousness God attributes to us and that carries weight before God. Luther often stressed, however, that he did not receive his theology through some moment of enlightenment; he had to work on it throughout his life. The real turning point for the Reformation, however, took place in 1518, for it was then that Luther came to the conclusion that the Word of God alone is the only means of grace and that it can only be accepted through faith. The related fourfold "alone," namely, Scripture alone, grace alone, faith alone and Christ alone (*sola scriptura, sola gratia, sola fide,* and *solus Christus*) is essentially the key insight behind the Reformation. By 1518, therefore, the Reformation had reached a point of no turning back.

In 1513 Luther held his first lectures in biblical exegesis on the Psalms. He sought to make the Psalms comprehensible by relating them to Christ. After he completed his lectures on the Psalms in 1515 he came to his second major lecture series in 1515–1516 on Paul's Letter to the Romans. Already here

his Reformation insight can be seen when, for example, he says, "For the righteousness of God is the cause of salvation. And here again, by the righteousness
of God we must not understand the righteousness by which he is righteous in
himself but the righteousness by which we are made righteous by God. This
happens through faith and in the Gospel."[10] Following his lectures on the Letter
to the Romans, Luther held lectures on the letters to the Galatians and to the
Hebrews.

Theologically Luther was influenced during this period by the mysticism of
the Middle Ages, for instance, by Bernard of Clairvaux (1090–1153) who was
highly respected within his order, and by the *Theologia deutsch*, an anonymous
mystical writing of the fifteenth century, Luther edited twice for publication
and for which he wrote a foreword in 1518. He also valued the insights of
Johannes Tauler, the fourteenth-century Dominican mystic.

Within his order Luther gained increasing recognition. In the autumn of
1511 he was made preacher of his monastery and in 1514 was additionally
called to be preacher in the parish church of Wittenberg. In 1512 he was made
vice-prior of his monastery and dean of its general program of studies. Finally,
in 1515 he was named district supervisor of the ten or eleven monasteries of his
order in Saxony.

Luther took all these responsibilities very seriously. The reform of the
universities was also important to him, as shown in a letter he wrote in the
spring of 1517 to Johann Lang in Erfurt, his fellow Augustinian and friend:

> Our theology and St. Augustine are progressing well, and with God's help rule
> at our university. Aristotle is gradually falling from his throne, and his final
> doom is only a matter of time. It is amazing how the lectures on the *Sentences*
> are disdained. Indeed no one can expect to have any students if he does not
> want to teach this theology, that is, lecture on the Bible or on St. Augustine or
> another teacher of ecclesiastical eminence.[11]

In the matter of university reform, Luther was supported by the private
secretary and court preacher of the elector Frederick the Wise, George
Burkhardt, who because he came form the town of Spalt near Nuremburg,
named himself Spalatin. Especially significant is the fact that Spalatin won the
elector over to Luther's side. Through his efforts toward university reform and
through Spalatin Luther also came into contact with humanism, which he especially valued because of its emphasis upon the biblical languages of Greek and
Hebrew.

In his September 1517 disputation, "On Scholastic Theology," Luther
parted ways decisively with Aristotle. Of greater historical importance,
however, is October 31, 1517, the day before All Saints on which Luther tacked

his famous Ninety-five Theses to the north door of the castle church in Wittenberg. This church door was, so to speak, the bulletin board of the university on which notices were normally placed. Luther, who likely wrote out the Ninety-five Theses by hand, challenged learned persons from Wittenberg and other locations to an academic debate over the value of indulgences. Those who could not come were asked to respond in writing.

On the same day Luther sent a letter to Archbishop Albrecht of Mainz in which he asked him to admonish Tetzel to stop preaching indulgences and to revoke his own instructions concerning indulgences. Along with the letter Luther included a copy of his Ninety-five Theses so that Albrecht could see how dubious was his belief in indulgences, traditionally related to the Sacrament of Penance. Since the eleventh century, the so-called works of penance were prescribed immediately following the spoken absolution and were understood as a means to reduce temporal punishment, including the punishments of purgatory. Theologically, indulgences were explained to be efficacious on the basis of the surplus good works of Christ and the saints who had done more than was necessary for their own salvation. The church, as the administrator of this treasure, understood itself as being able to distribute these surplus merits among the penitent faithful.

The income from the sale of letters of indulgence, that is, the certificates that verified that a specific number of years of penance in purgatory had been canceled, was increasingly applied to cultural and social projects. Hence the elector Frederick made use of indulgence money to support his university and to build a bridge over the river Elbe. What Albrecht of Mainz had in mind, however, was particularly questionable from a moral point of view. He was not only archbishop of Magdeburg and administrator of the bishopric of Halberstadt, but he also had become the archbishop of Mainz, thereby gaining the title and status of an elector and a cardinal. Such a holding of multiple offices, however, was forbidden by ecclesiastical law. For this reason he had to acquire the appropriate dispensation from Pope Leo X and pay the normal fees required to hold these new positions. Because he was not able to raise from his own resources the enormous sum required for the deal (that would today be close to one million U.S. dollars), he borrowed the money from the rich merchant family, the Fuggers, in Augsburg. To pay back this money, the pope allowed him to sell indulgences in his own territories. Half of the money raised was to be used for the building of St. Peter's in Rome. Because Pope Leo X was himself, however, continually in financial difficulty, a portion of this money came to him personally. The other half was collected as it came in by a representative of the Fuggers and went toward paying off the debts of the archbishop.

Albrecht was able to acquire the services of Johann Tetzel, an experienced indulgence preacher, for this work. Tetzel, a Dominican friar, had already been active in such work for more than a decade. Tetzel was not modest with his promises and boasted that he has already brought salvation for more souls with his indulgences than had St. Peter with his preaching. Frederick the Wise forbade Tetzel from setting foot on his territory because he did not want the money of his subjects to flow into other lands. Tetzel, however, set up his tent precisely on the border of electoral Saxony, so that many residents of Wittenberg were able to purchase indulgences from him. With their letters of indulgence in hand, they then came to Luther asking him for absolution on the basis of their certificates, without it being obvious that there was any real repentance of sins. Luther did not undertake anything until he saw Albrecht's letter, which promised the full forgiveness of all sins through the purchase of the indulgences. It was not necessary to show remorse or to confess any article of faith; one could even purchase indulgences for the dead.

As a responsible teacher of the church, Luther felt obligated to intervene. This was then the occasion for the formulation of the Ninety-five Theses. In his first thesis he explained what repentance actually ought to be: not a one-time act but a lifelong attitude toward God. Luther additionally contended that penance cannot be limited to the sacramental act. Also, the pope is not able to forgive sins but rather only to declare that they have been forgiven by God. Of course it was the furthest thing from Luther's mind to attack the pope, since at the time he believed that the pope would do the right thing if he were aware of what was actually taking place. Because the anticipated formal debate never took place and Archbishop Albrecht didn't show any sign of response, Luther sent copies of the theses to several influential people. To his great surprise, the theses immediately appeared in print and were spread rapidly over all of Germany, "as if the angels themselves were the messengers," as Friedrich Myconius, a contemporary of Luther, wrote.[12] In gratitude, Albrecht Dürer even sent him a collection of wood engravings and copper etchings.

Tetzel, however, was convinced that the heretic Luther would be burned within three weeks and his ashes sent to heaven in a bathing cap. Even Dr. Johann Eck, to Luther's disappointment, attacked him and characterized him as a heretic and a Hussite. To produce something more useful on the topic for the German people than his Latin theses, in 1518 Luther wrote his "Sermon on Indulgences and Grace." Within only a few months, twenty editions, a total of more than 20,000 copies, were printed—a quantity unheard of at that time.

FROM THE HEIDELBERG DISPUTATION
TO THE DIET OF WORMS

In the same year a formal debate was held at the general assembly of the Augustinians in Heidelberg, which Luther, as a district supervisor, was obligated to attend. In the meantime Albrecht had already informed the curia of Rome of Luther's activity, and the Dominicans had also denounced him in Rome. The journey was therefore not without danger. The Augustinians, however, stood by their fellow member and gave him the honor of presiding over the debate. He took the opportunity to portray his theology of the cross as opposed to a theology of glory.

In Rome the desire was to quiet this monastic squabble with Luther as quickly and discretely as possible by summoning him to Rome. Even Tetzel had been brought forward against Luther and laid out his position in 106 theses on the occasion of his licentiate examination. There he defended his jingle, saying, "As soon as the coin in the offering box rings, the soul out of purgatory springs."[13] Although the Dominicans promoted Tetzel to a doctorate in Rome it was recognized that he went too far. The papal diplomat Karl von Miltitz gave Tetzel a dressing-down by threatening to bring charges against him in Rome because of his immoral lifestyle and his questionable financial practices. For Tetzel this was such a severe blow that he retreated to his cell in the Dominican monastery in Leipzig, where he died a broken man in 1519. Luther nevertheless felt sympathy for Tetzel and wrote him a consoling letter before the latter's death in which he encouraged him "to be of good cheer and not to fear my memory . . . [and not to become] a victim of his conscience and of the pope's indignation."[14] We see here as in other instances that Luther was always at heart a pastor, even to people with whom he seriously disagreed theologically.

The elector Frederick arranged that Luther would not have to travel to Rome but that Luther would receive a hearing at the conclusion of the Diet of Augsburg in 1518 before the papal legate, Cardinal Cajetan. As a Dominican, Cajetan already knew what his decision would be. He was nevertheless friendly to Luther but could not persuade him to back down from his position. On the advice of friends, Luther finally fled Augsburg by night through a small gate in the city wall and traveled by horseback to Coburg, the southernmost point of electoral Saxony. In the meantime, Rome sought to find other means to lay the matter to rest. Karl von Miltitz was asked to convince the elector to exert his influence on Luther. If von Miltitz was successful, Frederick was to receive the golden rose of the pope, and his two illegitimate children would be declared legitimate. When he was unable to achieve anything, Miltitz sought to negotiate with Luther. It was even relayed to the elector that someone from his inner circle, with the hint that Luther was intended, would be named cardinal.

Luther, however, would not budge. He would only promise not to write anything further on the condition that his opponents also remain quiet. The silence on the side of Luther's opponents, however, did not last long and so Luther again took up the pen. In 1519 he wrote no less than forty-two writings, ranging from sermons to an exposition of the Lord's Prayer and the first volume of his commentary on the Psalms.

, In that same year the well-known debate with Johann Eck in Leipzig took place. (Initially Carlstadt argued Luther's position.) Eck saw himself as the victor, because he was able to bring Luther to concede that even councils could err. Afterward it was felt that other universities should decide who was right. The Sorbonne University in Paris demanded so much money for such a judgment that even Duke George of Saxony could not consider the possibility, and Erfurt did not wish to venture an opinion. Many humanists came to the aid of Luther, but the theologians of the universities of Cologne and Louvain declared Luther a heretic. This, however, did not particularly trouble Luther, because these same faculties has already condemned the humanist Johannes Reuchlin, who sought to rescue the Hebrew scriptures from their neglect.

In 1520 Luther's most significant Reformation writings appeared: *Of Good Works*, *To the Christian Nobility of the German Nation*, *The Babylonian Captivity of the Church*, and *On the Freedom of a Christian*. Even Duke George of Saxony, an outspoken opponent of the Reformation, wrote to Rome concerning Luther's *To the Christian Nobility* that "although not everything in this book is false, it is not necessary that it come to the light of day, since it is not necessary that it come to a scandal. . . . If all remain quiet, then eventually even the stones will speak."[15] In this writing Luther characterized the so-called Constantinian Donation as a forgery. This document, which presumably dates back to around the year 800, claims that the emperor Constantine, after his conversion to the Christian faith, ceded the western half of his empire to Pope Sylvester I and thereafter took up residence in Constantinople (present-day Istanbul). Luther contended that the pope could never be the successor of the Roman emperor. The pope should not exercise secular authority but rather should be the most learned among Bible scholars and should concern himself with matters of faith and the holy life of the Christian. The entire church, however, was in need of reform. This had to begin with the mendicant monks and extend to the priests and holders of ecclesiastical offices, many of whom, for instance, had a bad conscience because they did not practice celibacy. The priesthood of all believers was also stressed, as was the need for every Christian to be able to affirm and defend the faith. As one could see from the Council of Nicea, councils were not called by the pope but by the emperor. This should once more become the case. In regard to the Mass, Luther held that the laity once again should have access to the cup and that the idea of transubstantiation, the view that bread and wine are physically changed into the body and blood of Christ, cannot be an object of faith because the Sacrament of Holy Communion is itself a mystery. Finally, the Mass cannot be a good work or a sacrifice, because the Last Supper of Jesus was not a sacrifice.

In the meantime Rome continued to actively seek ways to silence Luther. Through Karl von Miltitz, Rome tried to persuade the elector Frederick to extradite Luther. Frederick was even threatened with the interdict, which meant that all worship services in his territory would be forbidden. Frederick, however, responded evasively, saying that as a politician he did not understand anything of religious matters. He could not be blamed for not allowing Luther to stand trial before the archbishop of Trier, because he himself could not determine anything criminal concerning Luther or his activity. In Rome patience wore thin, and in 1520 Luther was placed under the ban in the bull Exsurge Domine. Eck had the thankless job of proclaiming the bull in Saxony and had permission to add other names along with Luther's. In many places, however, Eck was merely ridiculed.

On the advice of Karl von Miltitz, Luther wrote to Pope Leo X, in whose integrity he continued sincerely and naively to believe. Luther included with the letter a copy of his writing *On the Freedom of a Christian*, in which he put forward the famous paradox that while a Christian is a free master and is subject to no one, at the same time a Christian a servant to all and is subject to all. The Christian has, therefore, a twofold nature, namely a spiritual and a worldly nature. In spiritual things, the Christian is subject to no one; but in worldly things, the Christian is subject to everyone.

When Luther first saw the papal bull in October 1520, he thought it was a forgery. Finally, even Frederick the Wise began to have doubts and consulted the humanist Erasmus as to what he ought to think of Luther. Erasmus responded that "he has done much wrong who attacks the monks in their bellies and the pope in his crown."[16] In Cologne and Louvain the first public burnings of Luther's books took place. In Cologne, however, the enterprise was not particularly successful, because the students there supplied lists containing the works of Luther's opponents to those charged with gathering the books to be burned. When Luther heard of the book burnings, a notice appeared on December 9 on the door of the parish church in Wittenberg asking people to assemble at 9:00 A.M. the following day at the Elster gate, where in good apostolic fashion they were to help with the burning of the godless books of papal laws and of scholastic theology. After several works concerning canon law and writings by Eck and Emser had been committed to the flames, Luther stepped forward nervously and threw a small volume into the fire. Only a few noticed at the time that it was the papal bull banning him. On the next day, Luther began to hold his lectures in German instead of Latin, as he had previously done. Luther was ready at this point to break with an entire tradition.

Finally, his case was to come before the emperor. The elector Frederick was able once again, as was the case at Luther's hearing at the conclusion of the Diet of Augsburg in 1518, to obtain the assurance from the young emperor Charles V that Luther would receive safe passage to and from the Diet of Worms, where he was to appear before the emperor. Although the papal legate protested, Charles V held to his promise. The monk was to be allowed safe passage to Worms, was to receive his hearing, and was to be allowed to return to Saxony. Luther's journey to Worms resembled a triumphal procession, with the town of Wittenberg supplying a coach for his journey. After the various papal intrigues failed to produce any results, Luther finally appeared at his hearing in Worms. He appeared for the first time before the emperor and the other officials on April 17, 1521. He was officially questioned by Dr. Johann von der Ecken of Trier, representing the emperor, and asked whether a stack of approximately twenty books placed before Luther were indeed his own writings and whether he was prepared to renounce any of these writings. Someone requested that the titles be read aloud. After the reading, Luther admitted that he was their author. As to the second question, however, he asked for time to think the matter over. This was granted to him and he was summoned to appear once again before the diet on the afternoon of the following day.

Luther had prepared carefully, since he was not allowed to read any prepared statement at his hearing. He began by apologizing in case he addressed anyone with the wrong title, since he had spent most of his life in his monastic cell and not in royal courts. He then divided his books into three categories. In the first category were works of a devotional nature, in which even his opponents could find nothing to fault. One could not, therefore, expect that he recant these writings. The second category of writings were books against the pope. To recant these books would only strengthen the papal tyranny and would open a gate to further un-Christian conduct. The third category consisted of publications directed against private individuals who defended the tyranny of Rome and condemned godly teaching. In these writings, Luther admitted to often expressing himself more harshly than was appropriate. Since it was not entirely clear from his speech whether his answer was yes or no, Johann von der Ecken demanded from him a straightforward and unqualified answer to the question whether he wished to retract anything. Luther responded in Latin:

Unless I am convinced by the testimony of the Scriptures or by clear reason (for I do not trust either in the pope or in councils alone, since it is well known that they have often erred and contradicted themselves), I am bound by the Scriptures I have quoted and my conscience is captive to the Word of God. I cannot and I will not retract anything, since it is neither safe nor right to go against conscience. I cannot do otherwise, here I stand, may God help me, Amen.[17]

With this statement, someone had for the first time openly bound himself before the church to the principle of conscience. Everything could be demanded of a person except one's faith, for this was a matter of conscience. Nevertheless, it was often forgotten by those who later cited Luther that he stressed that his conscience was itself bound to the Word of God. Luther did not advocate a freedom of conscience in the sense of an autonomous person but rather for the person as he or she is understood to be ultimately responsible only to God. Even his electoral prince Frederick later admitted privately to his secretary George Spalatin that Father Martin had spoken very well. But he then added, as an afterthought and half in admiration of Luther, "In my opinion he is much too audacious."[18] The emperor, on the other hand, commented already on his first encounter with Luther, "He will never make a heretic out of me."[19] The day after Luther's second appearance before the diet, the emperor wrote what was both a personal and official declaration in which he placed all things under the protection of the Catholic faith and the Roman church. He viewed Luther as a heretic and did not wish to have to listen to him any longer. Nevertheless, he kept his promise and guaranteed him safe passage home under the condition that he not preach or cause unrest along the way.

FROM WARTBURG TO THE DIET OF AUGSBURG

On his return journey, Luther was "abducted" on May 4 near the castle Altenstein and ended up finally in Wartburg castle near Eisenach. His elector had sent a message beforehand to Luther informing him of the planned abduction but explaining that he did not himself wish to know where Luther would be taken, so that when asked he could answer with good conscience that he did not know where Luther was. Luther spent the time following his abduction as *Junker Jörg* (Knight George) in the Wartburg castle. He let his hair and beard grow long, and he carried a sword on his side and wore a golden chain around his neck. For his own safety he was accompanied by a servant whenever he rode out of the castle. The life of a knight and the loneliness of the Wartburg castle did not particularly agree with Luther. Yet he wasted no time getting to work within his Patmos, as he called the castle, an allusion to the place of John's banishment (Revelation 1:9).

In September 1522 the New Testament appeared, translated into German. It became known as the September Bible. For his translation Luther selected the language of the Saxon court, which was used by every prince and king in Germany. He thus made use of a German dialect that was easily accessible to everyone. The rapid and broad popularity of this translation was therefore only natural. Luther wrote introductions to the individual parts of the

New Testament, attributing varying degrees of importance to the different New Testament writings.

Luther considered Wittenberg to be in good hands during his stay at the Wartburg, because Philip Melanchthon, the great nephew of humanist Reuchlin, had been active there as professor of Greek since 1518. Luther was very much impressed by the language skills of Melanchthon, who went from being a follower of Erasmus to becoming a close coworker of Luther. Luther had an almost childlike trust in Melanchthon, even when the latter went increasingly on his own, often compromise-oriented direction. Luther, in fact, greatly praised Melanchthon's 1521 work, *Loci communes* (which has been viewed as the first Protestant dogmatics text), seeing it as almost a canonical book.

However, unrest soon developed in Wittenberg, especially spawned by Andreas Carlstadt, who felt that Luther's reforms were taking too long and did not go far enough. When Luther visited Wittenberg incognito in December 1521, he was satisfied by what he saw there, for the situation had quieted down. He had barely returned to the Wartburg, however, when the unrest began again, aggravated especially by the so-called Zwickau prophets who claimed to have received personal revelations from God. In the Augustinian monastery, the religious images were burned and the side altars removed. People even wanted to overturn the whole social order and to kill all the priests and religious officials. Although the city council decided on reforms, the unrest continued and affected even the university since many students were so distracted that they were no longer interested in their humanistic studies. Finally the city requested help, and against the wishes of the elector, Luther returned to Wittenberg to restore peace and order through the so-called Invocavit sermons. Beginning on March 9, on Invocavit Sunday (the designation in some liturgical calendars for the first Sunday in Lent), Luther preached eight consecutive days in the Wittenberg parish church.

Luther placed many of the reforms demanded by the enthusiasts in the category of optional matters, that is, *adiaphora*. Thus paintings and other religious works of art could either remain in the church or be removed. Only if people worship such things, however, must they be removed and destroyed, and even then this was only to be done by those with proper authority to do so. In this series of sermons Luther laid out the fundamental principles of his approach to churchly reform: patience toward those still hesitating and freedom in regard to external ceremonies. Luther also preached in other places on the matter of reform, even when on occasion this involved personal risk, because he had to leave the territory of the elector on occasion for this work.

In 1523 Luther once again took up his lecturing duties at the university and toward the end of the year produced an evangelical order of worship in which, among other things, he called for the introduction of Communion in both kinds and for the pastor to read the words of institution loudly and clearly while facing the congregation. In that same year Luther also wrote *On Temporal Authority: To What Extent it Should be Obeyed*, in which he encouraged Christians to participate actively in political life. He also formulated his well-known thesis of God's two kingdoms within the world: the kingdom of the left concerned with external order and maintained with force, and the kingdom of the right maintained without force through the gospel. The following year, Luther once again had to deal with the enthusiasts led by Carlstadt, as well as with Thomas Müntzer, who had turned the peasants toward rebellion for the sake of his utopian plans. In this same year Luther laid down his monk's habit.

The year 1525 was decisive for Luther in three ways. First, he turned sharply against the peasant rebellion. Second, he distanced himself from Erasmus of Rotterdam. And third, he married Katharine von Bora. The peasant revolt, which reached its peak with the publication in 1525 of *The Twelve Articles*, a manifesto of the Swabian peasants in what is today the state of Bavaria, was an especially delicate problem for Luther, because his opponents among the princes could very easily attribute these revolts to his reforms. If, however, he spoke out against the peasants' demands, many of which were just—for instance, that congregations be allowed to elect their own pastors and force the resignation of those who do not preach the gospel—then he risked turning the large masses of the peasants against him.

Luther viewed the unrest not as a politician but rather as a pastor. Therefore, he spoke out against the princes who oppressed the peasants to such an extent that they could not hold up any longer under such conditions. He challenged the princes to deal in a reasonable manner with the peasants. In *The Twelve Articles*, Luther admonished both sides to seek peace. He consistently rejected the option of armed rebellion. He contended that one should not be misled into rising against a government, even when it is evil and suppresses the gospel. The law should not be taken into one's own hands.

In the meantime, however, the rebellions in southwestern Germany, Franconia (present-day northern Bavaria), Austria, Saxony, and Thuringia continued to escalate. Atrocities were committed on both sides. When Thomas Müntzer forced the council of the town of Mühlhausen (in Thuringia) to resign and established a dictatorship of the elect, Luther felt that things had gone too far. Villages, castles, and monasteries were stormed by fanatical masses, plundered, and burned. All order seemed to be transformed into chaos. Then Luther added a new chapter to the second printing of his *Admonition to Peace, A Reply to the Twelve Articles of the Peasants in Swabia* and extended the title to read: *Against the Robbing and Murdering Hordes of Peasants*. He now admonished the princes that it was their duty to restore order. If the peasants were behaving as wild dogs, they must be treated as such.

In the midst of the unrest, which was now being put down with cruel force and through which Thomas Müntzer also was killed, the elector Frederick of Saxony died. On his deathbed, Frederick wrote:

> Perhaps the poor have been given just cause for such rebellion, especially through withholding from them the Word of God. The poor have thus been weighted down by us secular and ecclesial authorities in many ways. May God turn his wrath from us. If it be God's will, then it will come about that the common people shall rule. If it is not his divine will, . . . then things will soon change.[20]

Indeed, things soon did change and peace again returned. Luther acted in this affair according to his conscience without regard to his popularity. He did not recognize, however, that there may be situations in which a social class must rise up against oppression. His explanation of the distinction between God's two kingdoms could have also taken this possibility into account. Through the suppression of the peasants' revolt, the wildfire growth of the Reformation came to an end, and from this time on the Reformation proceeded in a more regulated manner.

In September 1524 Erasmus's book *Diatribe de libero arbitrio* (*Exposition on Free Will*) appeared. Erasmus originally had a positive impression of Luther, for he saw in him a legitimate critic of the dominant morality of the day, as well as a supporter of classical studies. Luther likewise held Erasmus's edition of the Greek New Testament in high esteem and used it in the Wartburg castle as the basis for his translation of the New Testament. He soon noticed, however, that Erasmus was unwilling to break with the Roman church in which he found so many advantages. For his part, Erasmus came to see a catastrophe in the making in Luther's harshly worded reform writings, and he did not wish to be drawn into this tragedy. His main concern was that academic studies continue to advance peacefully. Several of Erasmus's friends were able to convince him to write something against Luther. In Erasmus's writing on free will, he stressed the ability of the human free will to choose salvation. This, of course, struck a deeply negative chord with Luther.

Luther took his time with his response. Finally he wrote *De servo arbitrio* (*The Bondage of the Will*), one of the broadest and most thoroughly thought-out treatments of a theological problem ever composed by Luther. He began by complimenting Erasmus for being the only one to recognize the real difference between the Reformation position and the old teaching. All the other questions of conflict over the pope, purgatory and indulgences are secondary. Luther then came to the core of his treatment and rejected in the strongest terms the teaching that we have a free will that is capable of accomplishing anything toward our salvation. The human will is like a beast of burden standing between God and the devil. When God sits on it, it goes in the direction that God desires, and when Satan rides it, it goes where Satan wishes. Thus it does not depend on us to go to one rider or the other, but both fight over possession of us. A free will in regard to spiritual things exists only in our dreams. In this way Luther drew the battle lines. Although Luther showed himself to be open to humanism and owed much to it, he did not represent a synthesis between the thought of classical antiquity and the biblical gospel. Important for Luther was the Word of God alone, which, as he understood it, spoke of the unmerited acceptance of sinners.

In the middle of the year 1525, which was around the same time as the time of crisis and of decision for the Reformation, another important event occurred that left many contemporaries shaking their heads. On July 13, 1525, Luther was married in a private and unannounced ceremony in his home, the Black Cloister in Wittenberg, to a former nun named Katharina von Bora. The ceremony was performed by the pastor of the Wittenberg parish church, Johannes Bugenhagen. Two weeks later, as was the custom at the time, a larger celebration was held to which guests, including Luther's parents, were invited. This celebration was seen as the public and legal confirmation of a marriage and included a procession to the church. Even Luther's friends were not certain what to make of his marriage. For his enemies, the marriage of this former monk to a runaway nun was a welcome scandal. Luther did not take this step because he was passionately in love, and his concept of marriage was also very realistic. Already the year before, he had laid aside his monastic habit and preached after this point in his academic gown. Now he also entered into the covenant of marriage, thereby turning visibly away from the monastic way of life.

To the best of our knowledge, Luther yearned for the security of marriage and became increasingly unhappy with his bachelorhood in the Black Cloister, where he was one of the few monks left. He had already written positively about marriage and for years had contended that the celibacy of the priesthood and the monastic rejection of marriage, especially when these were forcibly imposed, go against the will of God. Because he expected an early death, Luther wanted to make a statement on this matter through his own example before it was too late. He had even challenged Cardinal Albrecht of Mainz that same year to marry and to transform his territories into secular estates.

Luther's bride, twenty-six-year-old Katharina von Bora, came from an impoverished Saxon noble family and, together with several other nuns, was forced out of the cloister Nimbschen, in which she had lived since she was nine years old. Luther was able to find potential husbands for all of these nuns, and was even himself on several occasions encouraged to take a wife—a suggestion, however, he consistently rejected. For Katharina, he had in mind the son of a patrician family from Nuremburg whom she was willing to marry. The man's parents, however, did not want to have anything to do with an impoverished, former nun. Finally he stopped looking for a husband for Katharina because he heard that she had already found a possible husband: either Luther's friend Nicholas Amsdorf or Martin Luther himself. Thus Luther wrote in a letter in 1525, "Before I die, I will still marry my Katie."[21] An interesting side story involving Luther's marriage was that Albrecht of Mainz sent Luther a gift of twenty gold gulden, which Luther refused to accept. His wife, however, was more practically oriented and accepted the money gladly. With his marriage Luther also fulfilled a long-standing wish of his father.

The marriage was blessed with six children. Hans, who was born a year after Luther's marriage to Katharina, later studied law and became a legal official in the court of Prince Johann Friedrich in Weimar. The second child, Elisabeth, lived only eight months. Magdalena, their third child, died at thirteen years of age. Martin, the fourth child, studied theology but never became a pastor. He died at age thirty-four in Wittenberg. The fifth and most gifted child was Paul, who though sickly as a child went on to study medicine and was court physician in Gotha. Paul later held a similar position in the court of the elector August in Dresden. After Martin Luther's death, the sixth child, Margarethe, married the East Prussian nobleman George von Kunheim.

Despite all his work, Luther enjoyed his family, a fact especially seen in the letters he wrote to his son Hans during his stay in the castle of Coburg. He also composed the Christmas song "From Heaven Above"(*Lutheran Book of Worship* hymn no. 51) for his children. Concerning his marriage he wrote, "God has willed and brought about this step. For I feel neither passionate love nor burning for my spouse, but I cherish her."[22] Luther always appreciated his wife even if it was not always easy for her to live with him, especially because he was most generous in financial matters and often brought home more guests than she was expecting. Katharina was a good manager of the household. Upon Katharina's marriage to Martin Luther, the elector gave Luther a salary of 200 gulden a year, equivalent to what Melanchthon earned and which was later raised to 300 Gulden a year. Katharina was also able to acquire a small farm, the money for which again came mostly from the elector. She raised many animals, including cows, pigs, goats, chickens, geese, ducks, and doves, and she also kept a small dog. Katharina also brewed her own beer and had a fish-pond. She keep exact records of income and expenses. Katharina outlived her husband by six and a half years. Although Luther was a very strict father, the family found much enjoyment together. Music was especially appreciated, and after the evening meal Luther often took up the lute and the family sang together, with Luther contributing his strong tenor voice. Luther, who was also a good chess player, often played games with the family and with guests.

In the years following his marriage, Luther especially devoted himself to visiting the various churches and other ecclesiastical institutions in Saxony. The economic and spiritual situation of the individual congregations and pastors were evaluated and improved where possible. To improve the level of knowledge of pastors and lay people alike, Luther wrote his small and large catechisms. The elector was, so to speak, to serve as emergency bishop in his land and to direct the supervision of the churches. This move, consistent with the political tendency of the late Middle Ages in which the secular rulers took on increasing ecclesiastical authority, developed from a makeshift measure into a permanent arrangement. The oversight of the churches in Lutheran areas thus became primarily the responsibility of the secular rulers. The regional Protestant churches of modern Germany trace their origin back to this arrangement, and their borders still largely follow the old political borders of the territories of the sixteenth-century German princes.

In 1529 the Marburg Colloquy took place at the instigation of the nobleman Philip of Hesse. The attempt was made there to reconcile the reformed position of the southern Germans with that of the Lutherans. Behind this effort lay the hope that if the theologians could speak with one voice, then the princes also would be able to come together and form a common front against the Roman Catholics, who threatened the Reformation. The colloquy concluded with a common confession of faith, which Luther put forward in the fifteen *Marburg Articles* and which was signed by all the participants. Huldreich Zwingli, the Swiss reformer of Zurich, came very near to Luther's position here. Some time afterward Luther recalled how Zwingli, with tears in his eyes, had said at Marburg, "God knows that I have no greater desire to consider anyone my friends than those from Wittenberg."[23] In fourteen points the parties were completely agreed. Only in article 15, which dealt with the physical of Christ in Holy Communion, were the two sides unable to agree, since the Zwinglians understood the presence of the body of Christ only in a spiritual sense, while the Lutherans stressed Christ's real, physical presence. Yet it was still hoped that the two sides might be able at some point to overcome their differences on this issue. Luther, however, was right when he said Zwingli had another spirit. Zwingli was more rationalistic in his thinking than Luther and was not able to comprehend how Christ, who sits at the right hand of God, could also be understood to be really present in the eucharistic meal. Zwingli was also much more influenced by humanism and therefore viewed Luther's commitment to the Bible with skepticism.

In the following year, the Diet of Augsburg was held. Clemens VII, a cousin of Leo X and an illegitimately born Medici (the wealthy Florentine merchant family), was pope at the time. Although his personal conduct was above reproach, he was interested primarily in Italy and had little interest in Germany. Additionally, the Turks had laid siege to Vienna in the autumn of 1529, so the emperor could not afford to risk any religious conflict in his own empire and was dependent on the support of all the princes. This situation proved advantageous for the Reformation, and the emperor promised to hear the judgments and opinions of all sides at the upcoming diet. Because Luther was still under the papal ban, he could not travel to Augsburg but instead had to remain in the castle of Coburg, the southernmost point of electoral Saxony. The other theologians, including Melanchthon, traveled to Augsburg with the elector and Saxony's electoral chancellor, George Brück. Luther participated actively in the events of Augsburg from the Coburg castle through the reports of messengers.

Melanchthon, relying on previous confessions, composed the *Confessio Augustana* (or the *Augsburg Confession*) for the Lutheran princes. Luther was in agreement with the content of the document but admitted in a letter to his elector, "I cannot step so softly and quietly."[24] On June 25, 1530, this confession was read before the emperor, the electors, and the other representatives by the electoral chancellor, Dr. Christian Beyer. The reading lasted approximately two hours. The emperor listened attentively. Even the bishop of Augsburg admitted afterward in private conversation with friends that what was read could not be repudiated, for it was the truth. The diet concluded, however, with a new confrontation, for the emperor gave the Protestants, as he put it, a final six-month extension of peace before he would begin to punish violations of the Edict of Worms (which forbade any prince to give safe haven to Luther and ordered that Luther's books be burned) as breaches of the peace. This act led the Lutherans to overcome their disagreements and to found the Smalcaldic League in 1531. Luther was forced through this move to view the right to oppose the emperor in a more nuanced manner. "Is it allowed to offer resistance to the emperor?" he asked. He answered, "I for my part as a theologian advise against this. If the lawyers, however, are able to show that according to their laws it is permissible, then I am willing to concede that their laws are applicable."[25]

FROM SMALCALD UNTIL LUTHER'S DEATH

Shortly before the Diet of Augsburg, Luther's father died, followed a year later by his mother. Both Luther's father and mother received letters from their son shortly before their deaths that reveal Luther to be a faithful son and pastor.

In 1537 an opportunity once again arose for a possible reconciliation with the Roman church when the churches of the Reformation were invited to attend a papal council in Mantua. Because it was not an imperial council but rather a papal council, however, the members of the Smalcaldic League declined to participate. Nevertheless, anticipating that a council might be called, Luther composed the so-called *Smalcald Articles*, named after the town of Smalcald south of Eisenach, where the articles were agreed on by leading theologians and pastors of Lutheran territories. The articles were divided into three parts, with the first consisting of those points on which both sides agreed, followed by those points open to discussion, and finally, those nonnegotiable issues on which all discussion was futile. Luther, however, was not able to participate in the discussions in Smalcald because he was suffering so severely from kidney and gallstones. The stones, however, were passed and Luther regained his strength. Nevertheless, he was frequently plagued by sickness during the remaining decade of his life, especially from pain caused by stones but also by severe headaches and depression.

It became increasingly clear that the Reformation was not leading to a renewal of the entire church but to the formation of a new (evangelical) church. There is no proof, however, that Luther became melancholy and abrasive toward the end of his life, as his opponents claimed. Indeed, the events of the last years of his life themselves speak against this.

The counts of Mansfeld increasingly were in conflict with one another because Count Albrecht III, the lord of the region where Luther was born, was involved in repeated strife with his brother Gebhard over the possession of the copper mines. Luther had already written to his "dear lord" twice, and in the year 1545 Albrecht announced himself ready to accept Luther's mediation. Thus Luther, Melanchthon and Justus Jonas traveled to Mansfeld but the negotiations, due to other circumstances, did not lead to a resolution. A second attempt also had to be broken off early because Melanchthon became ill. Finally, a new journey was planned for January 1546, at which time Luther was accompanied by his three sons, among others. It was very cold and shortly before arriving in Eisleben Luther suffered a fainting spell, which he held to be of little significance. On February 1 he was in good enough spirits to write his wife a humorous letter addressed "to my dearly beloved mistress of the house, Katharina Luther, a doctor, the lady of Zölsdorf [and] of the pig market, and whatever else she is capable of being." He signed the letter: "Your loving Martin Luther, who has grown old."[26]

On February 14 he announced his return to Wittenberg since the negotiations were nearly completed. On the 15th he had to cut short his sermon because of a dizzy spell. But the negotiations finally came to an end on February 17 and Luther was able to sign the agreement he had helped to mediate. He returned afterward to his room and later ate supper with his colleagues but complained of chest pains. At 1 A.M. he once again complained of chest pains and laid down on a couch. At this point the town clerk, two physicians, Count Albrecht and his wife, and several other people joined him. Luther noticed that the end was near. He thanked God that he had revealed his son to him and commended his soul into God's hands. Then he prayed three times:

"Into your hands I commend my spirit. You have redeemed me, true God. Indeed God has loved the world."[27] Afterward he was quiet. Then Justus Jonas and Michael Zölius, the Mansfeld court preacher, called out to him: "Doctor Martinus, honored father, do you die in the faith in Christ and in the teachings that you have preached in his name?" This question was necessary so that his opponents would not be able to say that Luther recanted on his deathbed. Luther answered clearly so that he could be heard with a "yes." That was his last word.

On February 22, 1546, his funeral service was held in the castle church in Wittenberg by Johannes Bugenhagen, who was a professor at the university and preacher in the parish church. Melanchthon, representing the university, held a speech in Latin at the conclusion of the service eulogizing Luther. Luther died almost as he had predicted. He had said just two days before his death: "As soon as I return home to Wittenberg I will lay down in a coffin and give the maggots a fat doctor to eat."[28]

Although Luther, by little fault of his own, did not always contribute to worldly peace, the last work of his life was dedicated to political peace. He led a great many people out of the anxiety and uncertainty of their religious beliefs into the freedom of the gospel. Even the reformation of the Roman Catholic church, which was begun at the Council of Trent (1545–1563), would not have taken place had it not been for Luther.

When we compare the brevity of our lives with the incomprehensible duration the history of the world, and when we consider the endangerment of our lives through the increasing destruction of the environment, then Luther's question, "How do I find a gracious God?" becomes comprehensible. When one only has the privilege of being a guest upon this earth, the wish to know whether anything positive can be expected beyond this earthly life is only natural. The Reformation theology of Martin Luther provided an answer to this question that is still convincing today. Clearly and simply, the answer can be summarized in the following paragraph:

Through our efforts we can neither guarantee our earthly life nor can we come into the enjoyment of eternal life. Only the almighty God, as creator, sustainer and redeemer of this world, can lift us out of the finiteness of our existence. There can be no talk here of we ourselves having earned something. Through the life and message of Jesus Christ, God made known that he not only preserves us in his grace in this life but that he also desires to provide us the fulfillment of eternal life. The appropriate reaction to this undeserved grace is our turning positively to God in active thankfulness.

Luther's thought and words had to do with the priority of God. God must, so to speak, always take the first step in order that we can take the next steps. There is no cooperation of equals between humans and God but only on the basis of God's preceding grace can humans become partners in God's worldly and sacred activity. Luther's emphasis upon the priority of God did not arise out of some strange medieval conception of authority but rather out of the concern that any cooperation with God upon which our salvation might depend would always be accompanied by a factor of uncertainty that could have fatal consequences owing to our human finiteness. Luther's concern was not for rational security for our earthly lives, which at any rate is impossible, but rather for a certainty of faith which is able to serve as the foundation for coping with the difficulties of our present and future. In this regard Luther put his trust realistically in God and not in human ability which proves all too often to be insufficient. This insistence upon the priority of God confronts us immediately with the question, how one can know God.

2

THE CORRECT KNOWLEDGE OF GOD

Right up to the beginning of the modern era, belief in God seemed self-evident to most people, because nature and human reason seemed to show the existence and work of God. With the Enlightenment of the seventeenth and eighteenth centuries, the blossoming of scientific knowledge and technological developments, and the "conquest" of the world in the nineteenth and early twentieth centuries, this situation changed dramatically. Humans have come to believe that all that exists has come about through natural processes. When the French mathematician and astronomer Pierre Simon Laplace (1749–1827) presented Napoleon with a copy of his five-volume work on the mechanics of heavenly bodies, Napoleon asked him curiously what place God had in his system. Laplace, full of pride, is reported to have answered, "Sir, I have no need of that hypothesis." God had become, so to speak, homeless, and theologians increasingly avoided making any connection between God and nature. The great twentieth-century theologian Karl Barth contended that faith in God must be entirely grounded in Christ if faith is not to deteriorate into superstition. Interestingly, however, an increasing number of natural scientists are now asking questions about the relationship between God and the natural order. Even in our age, largely ruled by reason, the conviction that not everything can be attributed to accident remains strong. The American mathematician and physicist Frank J. Tipler, for instance, has written a substantial volume entitled *The Physics of Immortality* (1994) in which he contends that all our knowledge cannot simply disappear within the vastness of the universe. There must be a final integrating figure, called God, in which everything finds its connectedness and meaning.

Luther would, of course, have agreed with such a natural theology, for he was convinced that all people possess a natural knowledge of God. Christ, in contrast, brought us a special knowledge of God. Luther wrote, "There is a twofold knowledge of God: the general and the particular."[1] That Luther attributed a natural knowledge of God to all people is first grounded in his comprehensive understanding of God. He wrote in his explanation of the First Commandment in *The Large Catechism*:

A god is that to which we look for all good and in which we find refuge in
every time of need. To have a god is nothing else than to trust and believe him
with our whole heart. As I have often said, the trust and faith of the heart
alone create both God and an idol. If your faith and trust are right, then your
god is the true God. On the other hand, if your trust is false and wrong, then
you have not the true God. For these two belong together, faith and god. That
to which your heart clings and entrusts itself is, I say, really your god.[2]

All people have something in which they trust and to which their hearts
cling, and that therefore serves as their god, be it reason, career, or family.
Yet no direct path leads from this general connection to some sort of god, to a
knowledge of that one who really is God. Luther wavers in his judgment of
this natural knowledge of God, because on the one hand he criticizes it as a
projection, but on the other hand he counts it as a genuine knowledge of God.

THE NATURAL KNOWLEDGE OF GOD

In a sermon from 1529, Luther spoke about the ambiguity of the natural
knowledge of God:

> The whole world names as "god" that in which humans put their trust in times
> of distress and trial, that in which they take comfort and on which they
> depend, and that from which one desires to receive all good things and that
> can provide help. So the pagans have done when they first made Jupiter a
> helper and a god.... Afterward they created many false gods based on their rea-
> son. The Romans established any number of gods that were necessary to help
> them with their various concerns, so one helped people in war, one was given
> this power, and another that power; one was to allow the corn to grow, and
> one to help in the water in case of shipwreck. As many needs, good things,
> and uses as there were on the earth, so many gods were chosen until they also
> made plants and garlic into gods. . . . Thus does reason describe god: god is
> what helps a person, is useful, and beneficial. One detects here that reason only
> knows as much about God as Paul attributes to it in Rom. 1:19–21, where he
> says that one knows that God is.[3]

Because God has placed this knowledge within the human heart, such
knowledge cannot arise from human reason. The Epicureans and other atheists
sought to deny this awareness of God, "but they do it by force and want to
quench this light in their hearts. They are like people who purposely stop their
ears or pinch their eyes shut to close out sound and light. However, they do not

succeed in this; their conscience tells them otherwise."[4] Luther emphasized in his exposition of Jonah, "Such a light and such a perception is innate in the hearts of all people; and this cannot be subdued or extinguished."[5] If pagans, for instance, called on their gods, whom they really believed to possess a divine nature, then "this demonstrates that there was in their hearts a knowledge of a divine sovereign being."[6] All religions, therefore, testify to the existence of a powerful and divine being. So it is that human beings are naturally aware that their existence is limited and dependent on something or someone else. We are neither responsible for our own existence nor do we fully control it. "Because of a natural instinct, the heathen also . . . know that there is a supreme deity."[7] Luther makes frequent reference to Romans 1:19ff., a passage he draws on when he contends that "they have a natural knowledge of God."

The natural perception and general knowledge about God do not originate with human beings, because the natural order as God's creation already testifies "that humans shall call on God."[8] To rightly honor God, the Jews received from God the Law on Mount Sinai, while the Gentiles were given the law in their hearts. No one is excluded from the natural knowledge of God, for "there has never been a people so wicked that it did not establish and maintain some sort of worship."[9] In light of the universal veneration of God, Luther always stressed that all people "have had a general knowledge of God."[10] But through what means is the natural knowledge of God given? Here we encounter first the law, then reason, and finally philosophy.

Knowledge of God through the law.

According to Luther, the knowledge of God gained from the ethically obligatory Law, for example the Ten Commandments, is shared by all people. "The knowledge contained in the Law is known to reason," explained Luther.[11] "For to have a god is not alone a Mosaic law, but also a natural law, as St. Paul says (Romans 1:20), that the heathen know of the deity, that there is a god. This is also evidenced by the fact that they have set up gods and arranged forms of divine service, which would have been impossible if they had neither known or thought about God. For God has shown it to them . . ."[12] Hence the Ten Commandments, according to Luther, belong to the category of general or natural knowledge of God, and indeed blend together with this knowledge in many ways. The natural law, which is found in its purest form in the Ten Commandments, demands the honoring of God in the first table (the first three commandments) and requires the love of one's neighbor in the second table (the fourth through tenth). Since God has engraved the natural law equally in the hearts of all people, we are therefore able to know him through the natural law.

Knowledge of God through reason.

Luther was very skeptical of the human use of reason and philosophical reflection. He knew that humans can also quickly find a reasonable argument that allows them to do what they wish and to avoid doing what God wishes. Likewise, he also held philosophy to be too speculative for it produced many claims about God that Luther felt clearly contradicted Scripture. Yet despite these limitations, he viewed reason and philosophy as originally good gifts from God that enable us to know much about God. Especially in his book *The Bondage of the Will* (1525), Luther stressed that reason is able to say some things about God. This reasoned knowledge of God is gained from the work of God, particularly the creation, and from God's rule, that is to say, God's working in history. This knowledge, therefore, did not originate with human beings but with God, who gave us reason in order that we might know God.

"God has planted such light and understanding in human nature so as to give us an indication and a picture of the divine rule and show us that God alone is Lord and creator of all creatures."[13] Reason, for example, opens the possibility of a creator and sustainer among the so-called proofs for the existence of God on the basis of teleology (the study of evidence that there is a plan in nature) and order in nature. Even the knowledge of God from those laws recognized by humans can be categorized epistemologically (according to the study of grounds of knowledge) under reason, for knowledge understands God's commandment and with it the distinction between right and wrong. Nevertheless, knowledge of God based on reason does not stand on firm ground because, as Luther well knew, people do not want to believe that God punishes sin, and therefore they prefer to follow their own thinking. They tend to compromise this knowledge and turn to speculating about God through their own rational reflections. Natural reason can indeed know, "that this Godhead is something superior to all other things," so that all people can call on a divinity.[14] Yet God-given knowledge is often distorted through human high-handedness and leads to idolatry, that is, to the following of other gods rather than the true God.

Knowledge of God through philosophy.

Philosophy, which Luther uses almost interchangeably with reason, also turns its attention to the created order and recognizes who rules the world. It knows that there is a first mover and a highest being, as Plato had already shown. Yet the will of the creator remains hidden from reason, for humans are so blinded by their sinful self-centeredness that they cannot see the world as it really is. Of course, the Platonists came to the conclusion through their speculations that

God is spirit and rules the world and is the ground of all that is good in the natural order. But they were so blinded by the sovereignty and majesty of God's
works that in their search for God they did not recognize him. Why God made
things the way he did and why God rules in the way he does are questions for
which the philosophers have no answers.

The speculative knowledge of God produced by philosophy also fails in the
end because it addresses the pure majesty of God, which is beyond human com-
prehension. According to Luther, speculative philosophy seeks to reach the
beyond from the here and now. As Immanuel Kant later demonstrated, this is
impossible because God cannot be reached from a human starting point. Luther
admits that speculative philosophy is able to discern some things about God.
Yet it often becomes lost in abstract speculation.

Intuitive knowledge of God through the works of God.

To this point, we have seen that God is understood by Luther as the
incomprehensible being who is all-comprehending. At the same time, however, Luther firmly believed that God could be intuitively known by humans:

> One cannot comprehend God, yet one senses God's presence, for God lets
> himself be seen and known by one and all and reveals himself as a good
> creator who acts for our good and gives us all good things. This is testified
> to by the sun and moon, heaven and earth, and all the fruits that grow
> from the earth. But it is not the creator's fault and that of his innumerable good
> acts that we do not recognize God, as if God desired to be hidden from our
> eyes. No, the fault lies not with God but with us, for human nature is so cor-
> rupted and poisoned through original sin that we are not able to notice, let
> alone know and understand God.[15]

It is not God's fault but our own that the experiential and intuitive knowledge of God from his works is so ambiguous. Human beings want to comprehend God from a human starting point and from the natural order. But because
of our sinful turning away from God, we are no longer able to clearly perceive
God. Nevertheless, the natural order allows us to perceive something of God
and reflects something of God, for it teaches "that there is a God who gives us
all things good and helps us against all evil."[16] This intuitive sensing of God's
working in nature and history is one of the roots of human religiosity and of
the worship of God in the world religions. Luther agreed with the tradition of
the Middle Ages that one could detect the footprints of God in nature. But
what is the extent of such knowledge of God?

Speculative reason was able to come to the conclusion that God can do all things. But this fact does not yet tell us anything about the direction and intention of God's working. Through reason one can determine the attributes of God, but we cannot thereby know God's will. The recognition of the power and solemnity of God is fundamental to all religion, for it is written in the heart of every person that God is all-powerful and all-knowing. Further, they are able to recognize the justice of God. One does not worship God as an impersonal highest being, but rather seeks to enter into a dialogue with God that involves calling upon and being received by God. "Therefore all people know that God is our refuge, and they implore God's help and protection."[17] In the hearts of all people, therefore, the knowledge is planted that God helps and upholds those in distress and in crisis. Nevertheless, this God-given knowledge, according to Luther, has been wrongly interpreted, for these deeds are not attributed to the true God but rather to false objects, namely idols. People can indeed be monotheists (that is, believe rightly that there is but one God), but this too can be twisted so they worship a false god. The knowledge that there is but one God who is just, helps in time of need, and guides and rules all things is not accorded to God but is transferred to a pseudo-god or an idol.

We encounter here, according to Luther, a threefold limitation of a general knowledge of God: First, without the self-revelation of God in Jesus Christ, the knowledge of God is subjective, for it lacks the corrective of the revelatory Christ-event. Second, the knowledge of God is threatened by the sinful efforts of human beings to change the true knowledge of God through their own wishes or conceptions. Finally, the general knowledge of God, in view of the revelation of God in Jesus Christ, is only a preliminary stage on our way to God. General knowledge is replaced by a better alternative. Those who continue to follow general knowledge search for a God of their own wishes and desires, and not the true God who reveals himself finally in Jesus Christ.

Subjectivity of the general knowledge of God.

According to Luther, the subjective character of the natural knowledge of God is its greatest obstacle. Because everyone pictures God as he or she sees fit, the result is the diverse human forms of worship, because "as each one shapes a god for himself, so he also worships."[18]

Similarly natural law, which is supposed to be binding for our ethical behavior, is interpreted in different and often contradictory ways. Some consider good what others despise as bad and vice versa, for the orders established by God can be understood in very different ways. In Luther's view, God always encounters us just as we imagine God to be. If we think, for example, that God is angry, then so God is for us. "The God you believe in is the God you have. If you believe God is gracious and merciful, so will you have God."[19] The general knowledge of God, therefore, adapts itself to our own subjective conceptions, so God becomes what one trusts in and what brings one happiness. With this we find ourselves standing before a subjective projection of God. That does not mean, however, that God adapts to suit our wishes; it means only that our conceptions of God are changeable. Instead of trusting in God, we believe in a God of our own wishful thinking. Hence it is, according to Luther, of utmost importance, to have "a correct and proper feeling about God."[20]

The fact that we believe in God is not decisive, but rather what matters most is that we believe rightly in God, or, what for Luther was the same thing, that we believe in the right God. The danger of subjectivism in a general knowledge is that this knowledge is not guided by God but is instead adjusted to one's own desires. For Luther, an example of this is to be found in pagans, who "did not worship this divinity untouched [that is, the deity as manifested to them] but changed and adjusted it to their desires and needs."[21] Because the general knowledge of God has no corrective outside the created order, it usually proclaims as God a projection of human wishes.

The limits of a general knowledge of God.

As Luther continually emphasized, everyone has a natural knowledge of God, but a knowledge we usually make use of in such a way that it leads to a caricature of God. Our sense and understanding transforms our knowledge about God into a fantasized picture. The idolatry that follows from this is a distortion of the true religion, which led Luther to comment sarcastically, "Religion, however, is the greatest of all human achievements."[22] Because human reason does not let itself be led by God its knowledge of God is consequently false and inappropriate. In this way, religion degenerates into pseudo-religion, and the worship of God becomes nothing more than the veneration of idols. Luther would therefore agree with the thesis that all peoples originally had one religion. Yet this religion fragmented and degenerated into various individual religions. In regard to a genuine knowledge of God in today's religions, one can speak only of generally held fundamental conceptions but not of concrete details.

Because of our alienation from God, we cannot correctly interpret God's work in the world. We tend to confuse cause and effect and to see ourselves, instead of God, as the author of what is actually the work of God. Human beings often attribute to themselves what is the work of God alone while at the same time they view their own work as coming from God. The work of God, however, should not be difficult to recognize, for it always aims at sustaining and seeks what is good for us humans. Yet because God in the work of sustaining uses all creatures as instruments, through whom and with whom God works in the world, humans are often lead to the false assumption that they themselves are the authors of this work. Also, in observing the natural order, humans often conclude that everything takes place by natural means and that nature is grounded in itself. The sinful alienation of human beings from God has already progressed so far that they do not see God at work but see events as caused by earthly forces. God, in the process, becomes superfluous. Because the natural knowledge of God is prone to so many misunderstandings, it cannot serve as the starting point of faith for Luther.

THE SPECIAL KNOWLEDGE OF GOD

According to Luther, the Christian has only one appropriate knowledge of God, namely God's Word, which took on human form in Jesus Christ. Luther writes that Christ is like God because "he does not desire that you wander all over looking for him, but where the Word is, there you should go; and so you grasp God correctly. Otherwise you tempt God and fall prey to idolatry. For this reason he has given us a particular manner and place to seek and find him, namely through the Word."[23] Luther rejects the natural knowledge of God for Christians when he says, "It is extremely dumb to want to endeavor to know him. Therefore one should remain with the Word."[24] Seen from the perspective of Christian faith, the natural knowledge of God is able to tell us very little. "If God had wished to be known to us through reason, then God would not have come to us in the flesh."[25] Through the revelation in Christ, the knowledge of God has taken on a new and deeper dimension because, as Luther writes in his exposition of the Book of Jonah, a great advantage is to be seen is this manner of revelation, "So there is a vast difference between knowing that there is a God and knowing who or what God is. Nature knows the former—it is inscribed in everybody's heart; the latter is taught only by the Holy Spirit."[26]

The knowledge of God through the revelatory Christ-event takes place through God alone. God becomes human and thereby is able to be known by us, yet as the object of our knowledge he remains always God. God appears to us in a concrete human form. For Luther, revelation in this context implies first the self-communication and embodiment of God. The logical premise that something can only be known by what is similar to it remains valid here. God takes the initiative in both the act of revelation and in our acknowledgement of that revelation. Revelation is not a lesson about God that relates to us certain facts about God, but rather a self-manifestation in which God makes himself known. God reveals himself either in human hearts or in an external word. According to Luther, the revelation in the human heart is not a mystical indwelling of God but is comparable to the knowledge that God has taken on human form. God does not, however, reveal himself in such a way that God is fully absorbed into this revelation, for despite becoming human, God does not leave heaven."[27] It is not only revealed to us that God is and what attributes God has, but God opens to us his internal and otherwise unfathomable being. In contrast to the general knowledge of God, this knowledge does not remain knowledge of God's external being.

In the self-revelation of God, what is without limits is made concrete in bodily form. God is not comprehensible but lets himself be comprehended. In an analogy to the real presence of Christ in Holy Communion, in which the living Christ is present in bread and wine, the omnipresent God becomes visible to us in the revelatory Christ-event in a specific place. What is finite is enabled to take up the infinite into itself. Humans find God, therefore, in visible form in the historical revelation of the Christ-event. When God manifests himself he must at the same time enter into the created order, into the categories of space and time, to encounter us beneath the mere "outward appearance" of that work.

Incarnation as God's entry point into history.

The almighty, infinite God came in the incarnation of Jesus Christ into our finite world. For this reason Luther calls the incarnation God's greatest work, which contradicts all the rules of human logic. The life of Jesus is the center point of God's revelation, for in a unique, historical event, in the form of a concrete, historical person, the eternal one has entered into history. The place where we can comprehend God is not in nature, as pantheism claims, but in the life of a single, historical person. The humanity of Jesus becomes our point of access to the unknowable transcendence of God. God becomes knowable for us by entering into creation in space and time; that is, where God works in the natural order and where we are able to know God.

When God becomes a part of human history, God also comes into contact with our sinful alienation from him. Yet God does not become sinful, God instead deals with our sins. Jesus Christ, as the wholly other, stands completely on our side to bring God to us. Jesus Christ lives in God's order, which has been distorted through the anti-godly powers of destruction. So through Jesus, God can come close enough to us that we are able to recognize him. Because God takes on human form in his self-disclosure, anthropomorphic characteristics of this revelation are unavoidable.

Anthropomorphic characteristics of God's self-disclosure.

God has not changed in his self-revelation. To accommodate our finite nature, which is alienated from God and which the infinite God cannot accept, he has revealed himself in the incarnation in a way that is appropriate to human beings. For this reason, we make use of anthropomorphic concepts to describe God's activity. For instance, God speaks to us in a friendly manner, is happy, sad, or suffers, as can especially be seen in the Old Testament (which Luther interprets christocentrically, that is, as pointing to Christ). We must necessarily speak of the works of God using human concepts, or else remain silent. This does not mean that God becomes a new being in his revelation, but rather that he shows himself to us as he is and always has been in his hidden, transcendent being.

This revelation is not a depiction of God in which God still remains hidden, for God remains himself (*deus ipse*). God does not exhaust himself in his self-revelation but still meets us in his almighty sovereignty as the mysterious God, as the *deus absconditus*. The revealed God (*deus revelatus*), who desires to bring us into his community, is to be distinguished from the unfathomable God, who causes in many people not only confusion but also fear and despair. The distinction between God as he is and the revealed God guards Luther against the radical personification of the idea of God, which would mean that God, as the philosopher Ludwig Feuerbach (1804–1872) contended, is nothing other than a fully perfected human. God cannot be fully grasped in the personal categories we use to describe God. Rather, it is the other way around. One can make no concrete statements about the being of God but only about the Word of God. God is revealed in God's Word and in his Son, through which God manifests his loving will. What God is like in and of himself is neither of interest to us nor necessary for our salvation. Only God's self-disclosure, his Word, and the gospel are decisive for Christians. Luther had no interest in speculative theology but only in theology spawned by the practical life issues of human beings. This is to be seen in the fact that for Luther, all knowledge of God proceeds from God's revelation in Jesus Christ.

Knowledge of God through Christ.

In a table talk of 1531/1532 Luther declared, "True theology is practical, and its foundation is Christ, whose death is appropriated through faith."[28] Three aspects of this statement are important: 1) The foundation of theology is Christ. 2) The work of Christ is only understood through faith. 3) True theology is practically oriented, that is, it is directed toward the redemption of human beings. Luther, in an antispeculative way, centers his theology in Christ and the redemption Christ has wrought. Only through Jesus can one rightly draw near to God, for "the humanity [of Christ] is that holy ladder of ours . . . by which we ascend to the knowledge of God."[29] The unique position of Jesus consists in the fact that it is through his life that we come to the knowledge that God loves us. Jesus is the loving connection and the comforting glimpse to God. Only when we begin with Christ are we able to make appropriate statements about God and his work, because God relates to us through the unity of the Father's and the Son's will, just as the Son relates to us. We are able to glimpse the heart of God in the person of Christ. True knowledge of God is not speculation about God but rather the knowledge of God's will, which is made known in the sending of the Son.

Luther can even make the excessive claim that "the visible God was fully hidden to humanity before the advent of Christ."[30] It is only through Christ that we are able to move from viewing the hidden God to glimpsing the heart of God. From the action of God in Christ, we learn that God loves and accepts creation. Christ, therefore, is not primarily significant as preacher, miracle worker, or moral teacher, but as mediator of the divine redemptive will. Christ points to the goal of God's work, which moves unalterably toward its completion, toward the triumph of God's loving will in a new, purified creation. Yet in Luther's view, it is not sufficient to simply look to Christ, because others do that as well and then interpret him according to their own preferences. One must rather look correctly to Christ.

Theology of the cross as guiding principle.

In his commentary on the Psalms, Luther contended, "The cross alone is our theology."[31] He separated himself thereby from a mystical or speculative theology and centered all his thinking on the revelation of God in Christ. The cross of Christ becomes the center from which one views all theological statements. By adopting this approach, Luther did not follow the popular medieval theology of the imitation of Christ, but instead stressed instead the nearly incomprehensible outrageousness of the Christ-event, because this Christ has suffered in our place. The theology of the cross, which focuses on the historical figure of Jesus, including his death on the cross, stands in contrast to every speculative theology that consciously and in light of concrete human history seeks to make understandable God saving activity. Luther never tires of emphasizing that Jesus and his death on the cross contradict all human ideas about what God must do to achieve our salvation. We dare not begin with how God (according to our own ideas) must act, but we must instead hold firm in our thinking to how God actually did act.

For Luther, the theology of the cross has the same significance as our reflection on the incarnation of God. He contended in the *Heidelberg Disputation* that "true theology and recognition of God are in the crucified Christ."[32] If one wishes to know God, according to Luther, one must not attempt to force one's way directly to the majesty of God through reason but must rather focus on the incarnation of God. The sign under which the revelation in Christ must occur is the cross, for this is the work of God that destroys and condemns our reasonable considerations. God wills to be known in the weakness of the figure of the crucified Christ in order to annihilate our wisdom, which imagines God's revelation to be very different. The cross as the sign of the revelation of God also guards against deceitful imitations. Although the majesty of God can easily be counterfeited into a fantasized image of our own ideas, the cross will not be imitated or distorted by any religion, philosophical speculation, or our own fantasy. "One cannot love the cross," remarked Jürgen Moltmann, a theologian who follows Luther in this point; and what is not loved will also not be imitated. Therefore, it cannot be a human invention that God let his Son die on the cross in order that we might be redeemed. Apart from this, the cross of Christ also means that Christ, as a sign of his solidarity with humans, intentionally wishes to be weak to place himself on the same level as humans and suffer along with us on earth.

For Luther, it is an outrageous thing that God would be born as a child and die on a cross. One cannot understand this event through human speculation. Instead, God must lead our understanding if we are to recognize the meaning of this event. But whoever bypasses Christ does not recognize in him the hidden God. Such people are called "enemies of the cross" by Luther because they discard the value system of God. They label as bad the good of the cross, that is, the incarnation of God, and they call good all that is bad in their own thoughts, that is, their abstract, philosophical reasoning.[33] Although the cross looks unappealing, it is not something bad. Rather it is something good, because Christ, and thereby God, has made it his own and has destroyed the bad works of the exalted. Bad works, including speculative theology through which one seeks of his or her own power to fathom God, are those through which one hopes to stand before God.

The theology of the cross, however, points not only to the cross and the humbling and incarnation of God, but it is also for Luther an indication that God works under the appearance of the opposite. Luther is clear when he contends that, in Christ, God brought to perfection by destroying, that God made alive by crucifying, that God saved by judging, and that God revealed himself by veiling himself. Luther can name the cross the true negative theology.[34] God works like a dental surgeon who makes dangerous, difficult, and disfiguring incisions but who nevertheless does good work.[35] Even if one is at first afraid that things are only going to get worse, the surprising healing process comes in the end nonetheless, and the pain is replaced by a feeling of well-being.

Two aspects of this work of God under the appearance of the opposite need special emphasis:

1. All self-achieved knowledge of God is shattered on the cross of Christ. Luther once said that there is no religion in which reason is made to seem so absurd and stupid as in the Christian religion, yet he nevertheless believed in Jesus Christ. Through the hiddenness of God in his saving work on the cross, all the wisdom of the world is refuted. God wishes to be recognized only in suffering and to condemn all wisdom that seeks to comprehend things unseen with the help of those things that are seen. God must open our eyes so we can rightly recognize God's miraculous work, the cross of Christ, and its true meaning.

2. A knowledge of God that seeks to work its way up from us to God, or one that in contrast, begins with the mysteries of God, is destined to fail. God can be known only when we allow ourselves to be taken by God into his hidden work on the cross.

Why did Luther so strongly emphasize the hiddenness of God's work under the appearance of the opposite? He intended thereby not just to say that God does not wish to be sought where God has not revealed himself. Decisive for Luther is that in the revelatory event, God alone is the one who works. God chose the way of the cross to remain the sovereign Lord of all saving work and of the entire revelatory event. No one expected this event to occur as it actually did. Even the astrologers inquired first in Jerusalem and not in unimportant Bethlehem (Matthew 2:2) about the newborn king of the Jews. Yet God does not allow himself—or his revelation—to be grasped by any rational principle. Only on the basis of what has taken place can one describe it, and then only in approximation. But are we then completely dependent on faith, that is, on repeating what God first tells us, so there remains no place for reason?

3

FAITH AND REASON

It is often stressed that, according to Luther, one can achieve sanctification alone through faith, and that reason is described by him as a "whore." Luther, however, neither despised reason nor spoke of a simplistic, unquestioning belief in the Word of God. He was himself a university graduate and was well schooled in the use of reason and logical thinking. He also possessed a healthy measure of natural curiosity. He wanted very much to determine, for instance, exactly what took place when one fell asleep. Yet he was never successful in this. He would lie awake in bed, and suddenly he was asleep. He was of the opinion that death must be a very similar experience. "For just as we do not known what happens to us when we fall asleep and all of a sudden it is morning when we awake, so will we suddenly arise on judgment day, not knowing how we died and how we came through death."[1] He makes use here of his powerful gift of observation to illustrate a theological point. As Luther's criticism of the Letter of James shows, he also used reason to carry out theological critique. Since this letter nowhere mentions Christ, he did not believe it could have much theological value. (In Luther's opinion, this letter is on the fringe of the New Testament, a fact that many experts have since confirmed.) When Luther speaks of either reason or faith, one must also carefully note the context in which he uses these terms. Reason is, for Luther, first of all a gift of God meant to serve the fulfillment of earthly tasks. Because reason can be led astray through our sinful arrogance, it can only come to the right conclusion in matters pertaining to God when it is led by the Holy Spirit.

SIGNIFICANCE AND LIMITATIONS OF REASON

In *The Small Catechism*, Luther writes in his explanation of the First Article of the Apostles' Creed, "I believe that God has created me and all that exists; that he has given me and still sustains my body and soul, all my limbs and senses, my reason and all the faculties of my mind."[2] Humans have received reason as a part of their very nature from God. Reason distinguishes humans from other creatures, and because of it we are called to have dominion over the creation. Human reason is the source and conduit of all human culture; it is the

foundation of legislation, the arts, and human inventiveness. Luther can therefore say, "It is certainly true that reason is the most important and the highest in
rank among all things, and in comparison with other things of this life, the best
and something divine."[3] Luther also greeted the efforts of the humanists to
bring the sciences to bloom through the study of ancient texts and languages.

It is the regal duty of reason to serve this earthly life. It is the highest court
of appeal in the world and has the task of judging norms and putting forward
decisions concerning the correct order and administration of earthly things.
Even theology may not hinder it in these tasks, because theology neither questions the structures of public life nor discovers any new arts. Theology must
acknowledge the validity of reason in these areas and recognize it as a creation
of God. Yet it must always be made clear that reason serves only to this end:
that we might live in the world in an orderly fashion.

Reason as an instrument of world order.

Luther stressed that reason, "as beautiful and wonderful as it is, belongs
exclusively in the worldly realm where it has its dominion and its kingdom. But
in the kingdom of Christ, the Word of God alone has the say."[4] Reason is related to the world. But the Word of God, that is, the gospel, has to do with the
kingdom of Christ. We find ourselves, therefore, in two different realms of
being: in the kingdom of the world, which is ordered through reason, and in
the kingdom of Christ, or of faith. Luther makes a similar distinction elsewhere
when he writes,

> In temporal things and in those things that concern human beings, the person
> has enough reason and needs no other light apart from reason. Thus God does
> not teach in the Scriptures how one is to build houses, make clothing, marry,
> go to war, sail ships, or other similar things, for in these matters the natural light
> of reason is sufficient. But in divine things, that is, in those things that concern
> God—for instance that humans do what is pleasing to God and thereby
> become holy—in these matters, human nature is so stone stiff and completely
> blind that it cannot even to the extent of a hair's breadth show us what these
> things are. It is presumptuous enough to tackle such matters and to stumble
> into them like a blind horse, but everything that it discusses and determines is
> as surely false and in error as God lives.[5]

This distinction also demonstrates that the Bible cannot be used as a biology or history textbook. Knowledge in these fields is gained through reason
alone, indeed through the natural and historical sciences. On the other hand,
reason cannot dispute the fact that God created human beings and the world or

that history ultimately depends on the will of God. If reason seeks to make statements about whether humans are a creation of God or whether history corresponds to God's will, then reason, according to Luther, is overstepping its area of competence. Reason must restrict itself to what it has access to, namely the knowledge of the world. Reason must leave open the question of whether there are other areas beyond its own ability to logically evaluate that impact on our existence. When we speak of an ultimate meaning or final cause of human existence, reason can only examine the internal, formal logic of such statements. It is not able to take a position as to their legitimacy. We are confronted here with a distinction between the physical world that we can see and touch, and the noumenal world (the world in itself, as Immanuel Kant later described it). Our understanding and reason, in Luther's view, are much too limited to comprehend the world in itself and the majesty of God hidden behind it.

Reason that concerns itself with the world, however, presents its own problems for humanity. We no longer live in an original unity with God but rather in opposition to God. The self-glorifying sinfulness of human beings now impairs even the use of reason to uphold order in the world. For Luther, it is indeed clear that the logical, technical, and cultural abilities of reason have not been destroyed through our alienation from God. Even for sinners, $2 + 2 = 4$. Yet the danger remains that the person as sinner will use reason to further his or her own sinful self-glorification and, for example, in drawing up a bill, will egoistically pervert reason so that $2 + 2 = 5$. Indeed, Luther concedes that a sinful and godless person can be a good and upright ruler, parent, or business person. Atheists cannot be morally disqualified from the very beginning. Yet fallen humans are faced with the temptation to misuse reason. This can occur in a twofold way: humans can be untrue to their duty to live as God would have them live, or they can conceal and ignore the one who gave them reason and made possible their achievements in the first place. They boast of their own accomplishments and insist that they themselves have brought them about, rather than thankfully acknowledge that it was God who gave them reason. Reason is then misused for one's own glory instead of serving to honor and glorify God. Even Christians are not immune to this; therefore they require daily contrition and repentance. With non-Christians the danger is even greater, for they may consider the misuse of reason to be natural and are therefore not be aware of their false path.

In matters of faith, too, natural reason comes to totally erroneous conclusions. "Natural reason produces heresy and error; faith teaches and holds to the truth, for it clings to the Scriptures, which neither deceive nor lie."[6] That means that reason, as a substitute for faith, misses God and creates for itself a false god, rather than pointing to the true God. The reason of the self-centered person points to a fiction and not to the true God. Luther characterizes reason as a whore or a fool, because it lets itself be influenced by human intentions instead of unalterably leading humans to do what is right. Because reason is restricted to this world, and earthly reality serves as its final standard, reason stands immovable in contrast to faith. The reality of which faith speaks is, for reason, not real. Hence reason often seeks to oppose faith. This very possible dissonance shows itself even today, for example, in the frequent discord between the natural sciences and Christian faith. But scientific knowledge of the world cannot stand in opposition to faith, because the logical structure of the creation cannot oppose its creator. Only certain interpretations of this structure that are viewed in isolation can stand in contrast to faith in God the creator. The world (which is fathomed by reason) must not, according to Luther, be seen for its own sake but must always ultimately be connected to God as the source and goal of all that is. Only in this way can the question of meaning, which arises out of the world, be resolved.

In Luther's view, the essential correspondence of reason with natural law likewise leads human beings to forget God and to seek a this-worldly explanation for everything. According to natural law, which is directed toward reasonable behavior, there is a strict connection between cause and effect. Popular wisdom has expressed this with the proverb, "He who makes his bed must lie in it." If this causal connection were also to be applied to human salvation, one could conclude that salvation could be obtained through right behavior. Yet such a work's righteousness contradicts the preceding grace of God, through which God offers us communion with him. We ourselves can never work our way to God. Except for the wonderful reign of God, through which God gives us his grace, reason is closed off, blind, and deaf.[7] If reason wishes to address matters of the gospel, it must first be renewed through the Holy Spirit.

Of course, the laws of logic are valid as applied to the *structure* of statements of faith, even without the work of the Holy Spirit. Without faith and the knowledge of God, reason stumbles about in the dark in regard to the *content* of faith because reason is limited to purely this-worldly relationships and analogies. Yet by acknowledging the work of God, reason becomes a highly effective instrument for the faithful. Purified reason that recognizes its boundaries serves the faithful as an instrument for reflecting, proclaiming, and convincing. It becomes theological reason and helps us to rightly understand and expound the Scriptures. In this way, reason serves faith but does not abolish it by absolutely setting itself and its own constructions in the place of faith. In this connection, reason must not be seen as standing in opposition to faith, but reason's assignment to explain faith is meaningful and important. Faith, however, is not grounded through reason but through God. Reason and faith are both gifts of God. They must not be viewed as mutually independent of one another, but as dependent on God so they serve us in a complementary fashion. But what precisely does Luther mean by faith?

CONTENT AND THE STRUCTURE OF FAITH

It is often tempting to portray Martin Luther as a pure subjectivist when speaking of his understanding of faith. This is supported by statements such as, "We have as much as we believe and hope," or "You have as much as you believe."[8] Faith seems to be nothing more than a projection of one's own wishes, as Ludwig Feuerbach claimed in the nineteenth century, believing he was following Luther in this point. This assumption, however, is false. Luther did not understand faith as agreement with particular articles of belief but rather as a total, fundamental trust in God. Faith is understood by Luther as personal trust. One has a much better personal relationship with someone when one trusts this person totally than when one trusts the other person only halfheartedly. Trust also sheds light on the relationship between believing and having. If I completely trust someone, I become totally involved with that person so I rely on that person in trust. With Luther, one must first of all distinguish between two forms of faith: so-called historical faith and existential faith.

Faith as personal trust.

Luther once distinguished between historical and existential faith in the following manner:

> I have often spoken of two types of faith. You believe that Christ is such a man as described here in the entire gospel and preached; but you do not believe that he is such a man for you. You question whether you have and will have such from him, and you think: yes, he is such a man for others like Peter, Paul, and the pious saints; but who knows how he stands to me and whether I should perform the same for him and put my trust in him as these saints? Behold, this kind of faith is nothing; it neither receives nor tastes Christ [in the Eucharist] and can also not feel any desire or love for him. It is a faith about and not a faith in Christ; it is a faith that even the devils and all evil persons have.[9]

Luther can speak very drastically to say that even the devil has faith. Even the devil admits that Christ lived on the earth as a human being, died, and rose again. Yet the devil does not combine this with an existential faith that Christ came upon the earth, died, and rose again *for him*. Because this existential faith is missing in the devil, he must remain alienated from God and cannot acknowledge Christ as his Lord. In another context, Luther says that historical faith does not save. One can believe very much, hold it to be true, and nevertheless have no existential relationship to God.

Faith, for Luther, is a deeply existential matter. Luther is not irrational, nor does he oppose reason. But he emphasizes the connections with one's own existence above the purely factual. This can be especially seen in his exposition of the Apostles' Creed. In response to the First Article, which reads, "I believe in God, the Father almighty, maker of heaven and earth," Luther says, "I believe that God has created me and all that exists; that he has given me and still sustains my body and soul, all my limbs and senses, my reason and all the faculties of my mind." Likewise, in regard to the Second Article, he writes, "I believe that Jesus Christ, true God, begotten of the Father from eternity, and also true man, born of the virgin Mary, is my Lord, who has redeemed me."[10] Concerning the Third Article, Luther writes similarly about faith in the Holy Spirit and in the holy Christian church, "I believe that by my own reason or strength I cannot believe in Jesus Christ, my Lord, or come to him. But the Holy Spirit has called me."[11] Faith does not consist simply in the listing of data but instead establishes the existential relationship to particular facts. This presupposes the personal Other that is the object of faith and through whom faith is made possible, strengthened, and guided. Because God and Christ are not immediately and physically present, our faith is oriented in the first instance toward the Word.

Word of God and faith.

One cannot comprehend Luther's understanding of faith without considering the Word of God; they are inseparable. God calls us to faith through the Word, and God works faith through it, while at the same time faith is directed by this same Word. God can only be rightly known through the Word. According to Luther true faith can only be directed toward God, for it is God alone whom we can believe absolutely. Faith is trust in God. When we give ourselves unconditionally to God, then God will really be treated as God, namely as the one with whom an unlimited relationship of trust is possible. If we reserve a certain area for ourselves and shut God out of it, then we are like Adam and Eve in the story of the temptation. In the form of the serpent the tempter insinuated to Eve that she did not necessarily have to take God so seriously and could decide something without God's knowledge of it. With this, she and Adam fell from faith and from their trust in God. When we grasp hold of the Word in which God makes himself known to us as a gracious God, then God becomes real for us; God begins to be for us a living God and does not remain an abstract idea.

In the relationship between faith and the God's Word, it is decisive that God's Word always precedes faith. It is not I who seek my God. Rather, the Christian message first addresses me. My faith is not grounded on my decision or my searching but rather on the prior Word of God. Faith is not the result of human effort and is therefore not a human creation, but true faith is instead a gift of God. God speaks to us in and through faith. Of course, human beings, when they hear the gospel, are able intellectually and willingly respond to God with a yes. But faith is, for Luther, more than an affirmative confirmation, such as one might give to a weather report when one agrees with the forecast. Faith is directed toward the God who encounters us in revelation and consequently encompasses our entire existence. In 1522, in the preface to his commentary on the Letter to the Romans, Luther wrote, "Faith is not that human notion or dream that some hold for faith. . . . When they hear the Gospel, they fall to and make for themselves, by their own powers, an idea in their hearts that says, 'I believe.' This they hold for true faith. But it is a human imagination and idea that never reaches the depths of the heart, and so nothing comes of it and no betterment follows it."[12] Faith as one's own decision for God is a preposterous presumption. It would entail believing that we are able by our own power to turn again to God and to undo all the past things that separate us from God. Faith, however, is much more the invitation of God, through which, without our deserving it, God gives us again that Other whom we seek but cannot find on our own. Everything, therefore, depends on the Word, which God surprisingly and undeservingly gives us, bringing us into contact with the living source of our life. The Word of God meets us in our existence, which is estranged from God and makes possible and demands the answer of faith.

Luther continually stressed that no one can believe for another. Everyone must be responsible for his or her own faith. Yet faith is not an individual matter, even if Protestantism after Luther often gave this impression. The believer is never alone and is always part of a community of believers. This community is bound together by the members' common relationship to God. Not only do faith and God belong together but also faith and community.

Luther often identifies the Word of God with the Scriptures and does not always make a distinction between the Word and the words. This is especially clear in the disputes over the Lord's Supper and Jesus' words, "This is my body." Against all efforts at spiritualizing the meaning of the word *is* in the biblical text, Luther insists that this bread *is* Christ's body. Luther can therefore also demand a humble submission to the written word. His frank criticism of certain biblical writers or texts demonstrates, however, that submission to the text does not lead him to any kind of literalism regarding the Scriptures. Because Luther distinguishes between the center and the periphery of Scripture, he can take the Bible literally on one hand, and on the other hand can interpret it symbolically, according to the context of each particular text. It was only the later Lutheran Orthodoxy and Pietism that again "flattened" this contextual understanding of Scripture. Nonetheless, Luther has often been accused of having replaced the living pope with a paper one, that is, with the Word of God. This accusation is, however, unfounded. Luther did not hold faith to be grounded in any external authority but rather in one's own experience of the trustworthiness of the divine Other. The danger of a subjective faith is here ruled out, inasmuch as Luther never relied on experience alone but always had to verify this over against the word of Scripture. He also fought decisively against the "spiritualists," who despised the "external word."

Assurance and risk of faith.

Martin Luther wrote the following while considering the assurance and risk of faith:

> When you wish to say on your deathbed: the pope has said this, the councils have decided that, the holy fathers . . . have determined this, the devil will immediately bore a hole and break in asking, "What if it is not true? Could it not be that they have erred?" So you are pushed right back down. Thus you must know without doubt that you can say, 'This is the Word of God and there I stand."[13]

Faith is not interchangeable so that one can replace one's faith with that of another. Everyone must believe for himself or herself. The community of faith can only provide help and direction. It cannot be a substitute for the risk and involvement of one's own faith. Luther, of course, had many models for faith, such as the church fathers and the saints. Yet the difficulty of one's own decision of faith to trust in God wholly and without exceptions cannot be eased by such models.

At the same time, faith does not exist in isolation, because the Word and the content of faith protect Christians in their hearts and consciences. God's Word speaks to individuals and testifies to them in such a way that through faith every other mediating authority is eliminated. It comes down then, to a direct encounter between one's self and God's Word. Many people have spoken of a loneliness of faith in which the person as an individual stands before God without any protection or help. Luther himself had experienced something like this when in 1521 he stood before the emperor at Worms without any protection and openly confessed his faith. Luther, to be sure, stressed that everyone must confess his or her own faith and must bear the consequences for decisions of faith. But he also recognized the necessity for mutually strengthening and encouraging in faith. He mentions that the weaker our own faith is, the more we need the faith and prayers of others, so our faith will again become strong. While no one can make the ultimate decision of faith for another, it is nonetheless important that Christians do not stand alone in faith but instead are kept encouraged and supported through the community of faith.

Luther also did not understand faith as assent to what one is otherwise able to verify. Faith stands directly in contrast to seeing and knowing. God's hiddenness and faith are mutually dependent. Luther can even say that God conceals himself and his saving work to make room for faith, to which God calls us. Faith is not a substitute for seeing or for scientific knowing but rather has to do with another dimension is concerned with personal trust. So it is that all one's life faith remains subject to temptation, for it is beset by what is visible, by the empirical, and by evidences. In this world, faith is not able to take refuge in any "island of saints" and create a life of faith without threat and temptation. Faith, in the tradition of Luther, also stands in opposition to the methodological atheism of the natural sciences, which systematically exclude faith from their view of reality. In contrast with such methodological atheism, faith stands firm in protest, holding securely to belief in God as the ultimate source and goal of all that is.

Faith under assault.

The source of the threat to faith follows from the way God works in our world. In the first place it is not empirically obvious that God is *the* source that stands behind all things, because he rarely intervenes directly in the events of the world. Additionally, God always works under the appearance of the opposite, that is, in a way that we would not expect God to work. Such divine activity is ambiguous because in stands in contradiction to what one might expect. It is therefore important for Luther that faith does not fall victim to temptation and abandons God. Temptation and struggle are much more a school of faith that should teach us not to take the path of least resistance but rather to put our trust completely in God and to cling to God's Word. Even when God's Word contradicts what seems to be obvious, we must not give up and instead should hold on in trust to God's promises and to the previously demonstrated power of the Word. God's Word has proven itself and will continue to do so.

The experience of struggle and temptation (*Anfechtung*) also arises, according to Luther, from the law and gospel, the double form of God's Word. While the law is often identical with the visible order, the gospel brings what is surprising, unexpected, and often in opposition to the empirical. If we want to believe the gospel, we must at the same time believe against the law in God— that is to say, against reason and the empirical. One must flee directly from the word of the law to the word of the gospel, according to Luther, for "a Christian is the kind of hero . . . who deals with all kinds of impossible matters."[14] But such heroism must constantly be practiced, as Luther says in his explanation of *The Small Catechism*, so the old (timid and sinful) person within us daily is

put to death and there arises a new person, who lives in purity and righteousness before God eternally. While faith must assert itself over against empirical
experiences, it would be wrong to think that, for Luther, faith and experience
are always at odds and stand opposed to one another. The Christian does not
believe *despite* knowing better. Luther also knew the experience that produces
and strengthens faith.

Faith and experience.

Experience makes faith what it is. The act of faith is indeed a pure risk, a
complete reliance on the Word. One can compare the act of faith with learning
to swim. If we are placed in deep water, we no longer reflect on learning to
swim. We are no longer able to live from the theory of swimming but must take
a risk and learn to swim so we do not drown. Faith bears up, therefore, despite
all the risks. Luther is even able to suggest that someone who thinks his or her
faith is certain may not have faith at all. This person is living much more from
reflecting on faith than from the act of faith. At the same time, another person
who seems to be bogged down in doubt may actually have stronger faith
because he or she does not go into deep water with calculations but with fear
and trembling. Faith means to be certain of the Word of God but not certain of
oneself as a believer. But still, faith and experience belong together, because I
experience the fact that the Word of God is powerful over me, that it carries me
and does not let go.

Seen from a neutral distance, it is not possible to distinguish true faith from
false faith. Only when faith actually takes place is this possible. False faith originates from human beings and focuses on the individual. True faith, however,
originates from the Holy Spirit, who is at work in the Word. We experience true
faith when we are touched by it existentially. It is as if we are taken hold of and
led by God, and do not fall away from God as the true and powerful One, even
when we have doubts. We see an example of this in Luther at the Diet of
Worms, when he confessed that his conscience was held prisoner by God's
Word. The person of faith, therefore, is not autonomous, but rather *theonomous*
and subject to God's authority; such a person lives for God and from God.

The experience of faith, for which God and not some fiction is both object
and subject, does not remain unclouded. The risk of faith often seems to be
irrational. In this struggle, which Luther strongly emphasized and experienced
himself, he does not present any ideological slogans of perseverance, but points
instead to the empirical and historical anchoring of faith. In this regard, his own
baptism was especially important. With it he wished to show that he could not
be abandoned by God when God had already said yes to him in baptism. In his
dispute with the Anabaptists regarding the validity of infant baptism, Luther

comforted himself with the fact that God would never have let something that was contrary to Scripture stand for so long. Yet he admitted that such a historical argument was not unambiguous. He ultimately found an argument that overcame his doubts about infant baptism in the invitation of Jesus: "Let the children come to me" (Luke 18:16). Even one's own history can become a faith experience, Luther writes,

> At this point, experience must enter in and enable a Christian to say, "Hitherto I have heard that Christ is my Savior, who conquered sin and death; and I believed it. Now my experience bears this out. For I was often in the agony of death and in the bonds of the devil, but he rescued me and manifested himself. Now I see and know that he loves me and that what I believe is true."[15]

From the perspective of faith, one's own life history can be seen as a part of God's journey with us and as evidence of God's grace. The person of faith experiences in his or her own life that in the Word of God, Christ is present with his power and overcomes sin, the devil, and fear of death. Faith is not grounded on an experience that precedes it but rather, as a work of God, faith comes *before* the experience. First we believe the Word, that means we trust God; then we will see that this trust is not misplaced. What we believe even becomes the object of our experience. In the beginning, there is the hearing of the Word of God and faith in Jesus Christ. Then comes for Christians the experience of the reality of Christ in their hearts.

Nevertheless, the experience will not be an unequivocal verification of faith and of the fact that the risk of trust was worthwhile. As is the case with the love between two people one's own subjective feelings repeatedly interfere with the reality of the common bond. These feelings put faith into question and make us doubt whether we still have faith and whether this faith is in a living Other or in some fiction. The tension between faith and experience remains throughout a person's life. But it is not always of the same strength. Although there are ups and downs in the life of faith and in the certainty of faith, faith continually wins ground so that our own experience increasingly confirms our faith. The tension between faith and experience will only be broken when faith, at the eschatological completion of all things, becomes visible: "Only then will we be absolutely certain of what we have believed, namely that death and all misfortune have been overcome."[16]

Following Luther, one distinguishes between certainty and security. Ultimate security is impossible for the venture of faith. Nevertheless, the certainty increases so that the venture of faith is rewarding, because it opens for us a new dimension to God. Moreover, faith offers the only possibility of having of one's life guided by God.

4

THE DIVINITY OF GOD

At the center of Martin Luther's theology stands the divinity of God. In this regard Luther's thoughts are in stark contrast to our modern view of life. We desire to have an important say in all matters that concern us, from the question of whether God treats us justly to who will finally be included in God's saving will. Luther, however, had a very different experience regarding human ability and insights. Medieval piety, out of which Luther came, was influenced by a fear of God's punishment and also by the attempt to prove one's self well-pleasing to this God through indulgences, monastic asceticism, pilgrimages, and frequent attendance at worship services. Luther recognized, however, the immense difference between God and humans and between our finite abilities and God's omnipotence.

We can find no way out of our human limitations apart from God. Because even with the best of intentions our plans for our lives can only be partially realized, God is not able to build on anything we contribute. Instead, God creates where there is practically nothing already there. God is from first to last the deciding force in the matter of human salvation. This emphasis upon the unconditional work of God within Luther's theology is based upon his realistic assessment of humanity. If human beings participate in a decisive way in salvation and in the governance of the world, then their finite power and limited insight make it uncertain until the very end whether or not the intended goal will be reached. In this regard, it is characteristic of Luther's conception of God that God is not understood *statically* from the perspective of God's being, but rather *dynamically* from the perspective of God's will.

EFFICACY OF THE DIVINE WILL

Luther sees in God the supreme will that can have no equal. God sets the standard by which his own will is measured. It is through his emphasis on the will of God that Luther recovers a dynamic understanding of God, because the divine will is first and foremost action-oriented. God is always at work. God is not an inactive spectator of world history who, in deistic fashion, set the machinery of the world in motion and then retreated from the scene. Rather, God participates actively, decisively, and creatively in the events of this world. Luther does not understand this activity to be periodic or selective, for God does not take breaks and cease working but instead is a continuously active power. God is also active everywhere, so Christians need not fear anyone, because they are constantly under the protection of God's will.

God is almighty.

God would not be God without the power to carry out his will. If God wanted to, according to Luther, God could transform a stone into water, the desert sand into food, poverty into wealth, death into life, shame into glory, bad into good, and enemies into friends. There is nothing God cannot do and no condition God cannot change. God's activity needs nothing and presupposes nothing. Neither is God bound by the laws of nature, even though God works primarily within their limits. In *The Bondage of the Will* (1525), a document in which Luther especially emphasizes the efficacy of God's will, he writes, "The will of God is effectual and cannot be hindered."[1] God accomplishes everything through his will, God's counsel cannot be impeded, and God's will cannot be resisted. God created heaven and earth and is thus more powerful than these, even if many people do not believe it. No one can evade God's omnipotence, regardless of how ingeniously one might attempt to do so.

Luther's statements about the omnipotence of God could be derived from a theology of glory that seeks to shed light on the omnipotence of God through logical deductions and speculation. Already in the Old Testament and in pagan writings, Luther discovered such approaches, most of them arising out of a general knowledge of God. In the tradition of Luther, one might even say the knowledge of the omnipotence of God is gained not only from the revelation of God in Christ; it is also testified to in other religions and in philosophy.

But why does Luther emphasize the omnipotence of God so strongly? First, it is affirmed by the testimony of Scripture. From the Scriptures, Luther learns that God is Lord of lords. For Luther this is also attested to by the Hebrew word *adonai* (lord), a term often used in the Old Testament to speak of God. Through the miraculous signs in Egypt God demonstrated that "the gods" obey him and that he is more powerful than they are (as shown through the Egyptian plagues in Exodus 7–10). And when the New Testament speaks of Christ sitting at the right hand of God, this provides an additional expression of God's almighty power. Furthermore, Luther recognized that the assertions of God's omnipotence are a central theological and christological concern. The credibility of the First Commandment and its promise depend on these assertions, for if God were not almighty God would merely be one god alongside other gods. Even

Christology is dependent on the doctrine of God's omnipotence. How could Christ be the Lord of all if God were not almighty? Hence the assertion of God's omnipotence is not only an attribute of God but also characterizes the very essence of God. Through the knowledge of God made possible by Christ we endow God not with specific attributes, as in a general knowledge of God, but instead advance a knowledge of God's very being based on God's own self-disclosure.

God works everything.

The knowledge of God's influence is closely bound with that of God's omnipotence. For Luther there was no question that everything that happens on earth is under God's control. God pushes everything along, as it were, as an internal driving force. God's working is revealed first in nature, so that no leaf falls from a tree unless God wills it. It is revealed in the saving activity of God inasmuch as no one can obtain salvation apart from the effective working of God. Finally, God's working is evident in our daily lives, for apart from the will of God, we could not even eat or drink. God is even completely efficacious in the course of history. All earthly authorities rest in God's hand, and God can lead them wherever he will. Earthly leaders are not capable of thinking of anything unless it is suggested by God. Because God brings about and reigns over all things, God also holds power over the future. God alone knows what will happen in the future and can thus disclose the future to us.

This emphasis on God's working entails many problems. It encourages us to view God as a sole actor who alone controls all things. If God alone is behind good and evil, fortune and misfortune, God can assume demonic characteristics. This danger is not completely absent from Luther's line of thought. Yet Luther is primarily concerned with an important theological problem; namely God's authorship of all that is good. God, accordingly, is good, wise, just, truthful, and merciful. If we did not view God as working all in all and as a sole actor, then the divinity of God—in the sense that God is author of the good—would be jeopardized. God would then be only one divine power among many, and salvation, in an ultimately effectual sense, could not be hoped for from God.

But alongside this important theological concern, there remains the danger that the emphasis on the sole-activity of God will lead to a doctrine of absolute predestination. In his book *The Bondage of the Will*, Luther wrestled especially with the doctrine of predestination. The assertion that humans can do for their salvation only what God does in them appears justified, so long as we apply this assertion only to the matter of our contributing to our own salvation. But if the premise that God is a sole actor is also used to argue that some people are excluded from salvation, then the premise bears within it the danger that God will be made into a god above or outside of the law, and thus a demon or a tyrant. An additional problem of the doctrine of God's working is that one views every occurrence on earth as determined by God. It would then be only a question of time before this doctrine would be prepare the way for a mechanistic worldview.

These problems, however, did not present themselves for Luther. His understanding of God was not derived in a speculative manner but instead was oriented toward God who had revealed himself as the Father of Jesus Christ. God's sole activity was seen by Luther in the revelatory Christ-event, through which God disclosed himself to human beings and enabled them to understand his self-disclosure. Luther thus stressed the personal character of the revelation of God in Jesus Christ as well as the uniqueness of this self-revelation. Yet Luther was unable to avoid another danger that arises from the concept of God's working everything. With God's sole-activity and working of all in all, evil loses its potency because it appears as a sideline of God's saving activity. This dilemma has posed itself in recent times in the theology of Karl Barth (1886–1968), who also placed great stress on the sole-activity of God. If God influences everything, then it is difficult to avoid the conclusion that God brings about evil or at least works through it, and that evil does not possess an independent reality. (This problem will be taken up in chapter 5. At this point, suffice it to say that Luther indeed recognized evil as an independent anti-godly reality.)

The divine will is grounded in God's own being.

If God is continuously at work and is both almighty and influences everything, then the question arises whether God's activity is guided by certain externally established rules or whether God's will itself provides its own guidelines that inform the divine activity. For Luther it is obvious that we cannot inquire about the ultimate ground of God's will, because the will of God is grounded in its own self and is the ultimate basis for its activity: "It is enough to know that God so wills, and it is becoming for us to reverence, love, and adore his will."[2] Luther presupposes here the ability of humans to know the will of God and contends that we must submit ourselves to it. We are not to question—as people often do today—why God acts in a certain manner. Luther can even say that it is an abominable blasphemy to ask God why he does what he does, for in doing so one questions God and makes oneself out to be smarter and more knowledgeable than God. God's activity does not allow itself to be steered by our reason but rather is to be unconditionally acknowledged. And those things that flow from God's activity are to be used with thankfulness. It is also useless to ask about the hidden ways God governs the world, for in doing so one walks on the slippery surface of a speculative theology.

There remains only one possible response to God's activity: to entrust everything to God, conceding that God knows better than we do. But does not the challenge of Luther's demand imply an intellectual sacrifice, since in regard to God and God's activity, one must switch off one's reason? Luther would deny that this is the case. His primary concern is with the divinity of God. The majesty of God cannot be fathomed but rather must be recognized as an awe-inspiring mystery. Additionally, the attempt to comprehend the divine will is condemned to failure because the divine will and human wills are not analogous to one another. We cannot unlock the mystery of God's will by beginning from the human will, because the divine will is complete in itself and needs no foundation. If one were able to explain or ground God's action, the majesty and perfection of God would be abrogated in the process. For Luther the question about the *why* of God's action is pointless. One can only ascertain after the fact that God has acted in a certain way. The will of God is therefore always primary and cannot be grounded. God is not, however, capricious but rather has committed himself to our salvation through his self-disclosure. It follows that God does not act high-handedly or irrationally and therefore does not work in a demonic way.

God is the only necessary being.

The will and being of God are grounded in God's own self. Only God is necessary. Nothing else need exist if God so desired. All other being is distinct from God because it is brought into being by God. It is derived being, while God exists on the basis of his own being. God is the power inherent in everything and that establishes all reality. God does not refrain from doing what is within the reach of his omnipotence but rather works in everything. This view is essential for Luther's conception of God. He takes up from tradition the idea that God is pure act, but adapts this idea so that God is not a disinterested will but is understood as working in a strictly personal way. God is, then, unchanging and unchangeable within himself, God works continuously for our salvation.

God is will and deed, the constant "mover" of the beings he has created. It is seen here that Luther's dynamic understanding of God is oriented toward history. The contrast to speculative theology is likewise clear. Luther does take up traditional philosophical ideas, but he always conceives of God in personal terms because he understands God from the perspective of God's revelation in Christ. Therefore Luther stresses that God is not an abstract being but deals with us continuously according to his love and goodness. So Luther can even say that God neither wills nor loves sin. But when God is the only necessary being, this also means that God is always so close to us that we cannot fall out of his hand. God is always with us and deals with us according to his love. For Luther, God is not an impersonal fate or an unconcerned God of fatalism. Instead, God possesses the dynamic structure of a personal being.

God is truthful.

If God is the only necessary being and God's will is grounded within his own self, that does not mean God acts without any rules, for there is an important constant: "God is truthful," even if one is unable to show this empirically.[3] God's faithfulness and truthfulness are extremely important for Luther. Because God is truthful, one can rely on God's promises and place oneself trustingly under his protection. Every believer knows that God fulfills his promises and his threats. If it were otherwise, one could not rely on God and a relationship of trust with God would be impossible. We are able to trust God's Word because God does not lie and would be incapable of lying without becoming a demonic being. The distinction between the perfection of God and the imperfection of humans is clearly revealed here. The truthfulness of God is not a theoretical postulate but is made concrete through Christ who remained faithful to his mission. His promises, therefore, such as he spoke in the institution of the Lord's Supper (see Mark 14:22–25), are true. Hence God's will is not without self-restriction, and God does not do evil. This positive orientation is the foundation for our relationship to God. Yet the question remains open whether God is autonomous in his will, or whether God must, so to speak, inevitably act in a certain way.

The will of God is ultimate criterion.

Luther emphasizes that for God there is no rule, standard, or law, and therefore nothing God can violate. Luther illustrates this with the story of Pharaoh in Exodus 7–11.[4] The plagues that came upon Pharaoh were undoubtedly terrible, and had humans brought such suffering on him, it would have been an evil deed. But because it was God who sent the plagues, we must call these actions good. We cannot judge God according to the appearances of his actions so that these would become the measure for good and evil. A mistake made by many people is to claim that God has a certain nature or character and then to judge God according to these preconceived notions. By making themselves the standard against which they measure God, they offend God's majesty. According to Luther, it is arrogant to suggest that God does something bad, because where there is no law, there can be no sin. God is above every law and cannot, therefore, violate any law. Yet Luther admits that our reason is unable to comprehend this. God's will remains the supreme law according to which everything is measured and judged and to which no other standard has anything to add. No one can either judge or justify God, for God is the eternally constant and unchanging justice and the supreme judge of all things.

The free will of God cannot be unjust.

The justice of God is consequently not a principle attributed to God but rather is derived from the divinity of God: "God is not God because he is just, but rather, because God is God, he is just. God's divinity is his justice."[5] The actions and will of God are always correct and are never arbitrary. Although the divine will is not determined by external criteria, God does not act according to constantly changing standards. What is good and what is evil is not subject to arbitrariness. According to his own being, God is just. This is true even when, according to our human understanding, God may appear to be unjust. That does not mean God is a good principle that must always do what is good, but rather God wills the good and therefore also does what is good. God establishes good and evil through his will, and whoever acts contrary to what God wills is not good. Good and evil are determined according to God's will, but not vice versa, so one cannot ethically judge God's actions according to our notions of good and evil. God's will is the ultimate criterion for all things. The divinity of God is to be seen in the fact that we can learn from God's actions what is good, yet we do not possess any other standard by which we could judge God's actions as good. In this way the priority of God—a priority that is also to be seen in God's creative activity—is safeguarded.

GOD'S ACTIVITY IN THE CREATION

God creates and preserves all things, and nothing comes into being or continues to be apart from the active work of God. The relationship between God and the world is thus different from that between human beings and their creations. When a human-made product is finished, it gains a certain independence from its maker, for it can continue to exist apart from the one who made it. The world, however, cannot continue to exist for a single moment apart from the sustaining activity of God. Luther wrote of God's activity in creation, "He did not therefore create the world the way a carpenter builds a house and then goes away, leaving it stand as it is. Rather, God remains and sustains everything as he made it, otherwise it would neither be able to stand nor to continue."[6] This continuous divine work of preservation is at the same time an ongoing new act of creating. God is not yet finished with the work of creation but continues to further create. Through his active preservation and ongoing creating, God is present in all of reality:

For God dispatches no officials or angels when he creates or preserves something, but all is the work of his divine power. If God is to create or preserve,
however, he must be present and must make and preserve creation, both in its
innermost and outermost aspects.[7]

The creative power of God is directly present in nature and in the entire
creation. Although God is present in nature, God's all-present power is not
identical with the course of world history, for the power of God transcends the
world. With this distinction, Luther is able to avoid every form of pantheism.
He points out that God is not something with length or breadth that one could
confine to a particular place and measure. God is, rather, incomprehensible and
immeasurable, beyond and above all things, and at the same time in all things.
God's power is beyond all standards one might attribute to it. God's power is its
own dimension which is present in all things while at the same time tran-
scending all things.

The indirect involvement of God.

God's activity within the creation is seldom carried out directly or immediately. Although God is active everywhere, God works mostly through the
guise of forces discernible to us: "All creatures are God's masks and costumes,
which God wants to work with him to help create all manner of things, yet God
can and does also work without them."[8] God does not need any earthly cooperation, but out of his own free will God summons and asks for the cooperation of earthly forces. God wants us to accomplish our tasks with earnestness in
whatever situation we find ourselves. We should do this not because God needs
us, but because God has commanded it and will not give us his blessing without our own effort. Nevertheless, we should not view ourselves as truly responsible for the fruits of our labors, since God himself produces them. Luther
explains this in his *Small Catechism* in the explanation of the Fourth Petition of
the Lord's Prayer, "Give us today our daily bread." Luther writes, "To be sure,
God provides daily bread, even to the wicked, without our prayer, but we pray
in this petition that God may make us aware of his gifts and enable us to receive
our daily bread with thanksgiving."[9] Ultimately, all human success or results are
God's gracious action, so only in the foreground do they appear to show a causal
connection between our effort and our success. Through God's command and
promise, work and blessing are connected and related to one another. Because
the honor of authorship belongs to God alone, we may depend on God in our
labor: "Creatures are only the hands, channels, and means through which God
bestows all blessings."[10] God's creative will not only provides human effort with
meaning but also sets its boundaries. Without our active readiness to cooperate

with God, God doesn't give us anything, but our cooperation alone does not bring about the result.

Sovereignty of God's activity.

It is important to remember that God works everything through his Word. "His command or speech is equivalent to creation."[11] Through his powerful Word, God brings about, for instance, the change of the seasons, as well as the historical communal life of humanity within the political order. When Luther speaks here of the Word of God, he does not have in mind the gospel but rather the creative and preserving Word. Just as God called into existence what was not at the beginning of the world through his Word, so God continues today to work sovereignly through his Word, so no one can hinder or restrict him. Of course, one could ask whether Luther introduces a divine determinism that reduces all human freedom to nothing when he refers to God's sovereign activity in the creation. One must take into account, however, that Luther was an eminently existential theologian who focused on our approach to faith. In Luther's thought, the recognition of God's sole activity and God's working all in all has immediate implications for faith. If God is sovereign and continuously active, then we can put our confidence in what God promises.

Because God is active everywhere and in all things, we are always in God's hands. We can go wherever we wish, but in the end we always encounter God (as described in Psalm 139). This inescapable and living presence of God is for humans, depending on their individual relationship to God, either a frightening or a trust inspiring reality. For the faithful this means heaven, but for those who distanced themselves from God, it signifies hell: "He is present everywhere, in death, in hell, in the midst of our foes, yes, also in their hearts. For God has created all things, and he also governs them, and that they must all do as he wills."[12] Therefore we have nothing and no one to fear other than God. Those who put their trust in God are able to confidently believe that nothing can harm them. God's power in creation is the reason for the confidence of the faithful. They know that they are kept safe through God's works of creation and preservation. It is otherwise for those who do not put their faith in God. Ultimately they cannot rely on anything, and sooner or later will realize that their lives have no firm foundation.

Omnipotence of God.

God holds humanity completely in his hand through his omnipotence. Luther emphasized with particular clarity in his dispute with Erasmus in *The Bondage of the Will* that free will is an attribute that belongs to God alone.

Since God affects everything in human beings, they can only desire and do what God himself does in them. God is the unresting driving force in his creatures. For believers, this is a great comfort, because they recognize that even their faith in God is not their own work but is wrought in them by God. For those without God, however, his omnipotence is a frightening reality, for they are moved to act in correspondence to their godless nature:

> Hence, it comes about that the ungodly man cannot but continually err and sin, because he is caught up in the movement of divine power and not allowed to be idle, but wills, desires, and acts according to the kind of person he himself is.[13]

Luther even maintained that God can make the evil person even more evil, obstinate, and hardened. In contrast to this idea of obstinacy, which is seldom mentioned by Luther and with which we cannot completely agree in this form, we must remember that Luther, although he knows humans to be entirely in God's hands, views them at the same time, in contrast to God, as accountable and indebted to God and finally to be judged by God. Through this accountability before God the conception of God's working in everything is qualified.

Luther neither makes God's working in everything absolute, nor does he draw from it every possible conclusion. He would never claim, for instance, that God causes people to sin. Although God also works in the godless so that they remain the way they are, God moves them only in a way consistent with the state in which he finds them. In connection with God's activity in creation, Luther does not discuss where or how human guilt and sin originated. They are simply present and demand human accountability. Even the godless are not only moved by God to continue in their godless ways, but they are also preserved and kept by God as much as every other person. Luther has in view here not so much humans as God, on whom everything in which we can trust in ultimately depends. This is also to be seen in God's redemptive activity.

Redemptive work of God.

The divinity of God is especially emphasized in redemption because the human certainty of salvation rests on God's trustworthiness. God the creator is not only responsible for the existence of human beings but also for the accomplishment of their salvation. When we profess faith in God the creator, this includes an admission of our own inadequacy and means that we rely on God for everything. God's saving action occurs, as does his entire work of creation, out of nothing. The creation out of nothing (*creatio ex nihilo*) is not only a statement about the origin of the world, indicating that God works without prerequisites, but it is also a statement about the saving activity of God directed toward humanity. If our salvation depended on us or on our cooperation, it would be very much uncertain and would often turn into a disaster. With his emphasis on creation out of nothing, Luther points toward God's activity under the guise of the opposite. Where God will exalt, God first humbles; where God creates life, God first brings about death. God accomplishes a foreign work, an *opus alienum*, in order to bring about his proper work, his *opus proprium*. God's activity cannot be rationally predicted. Rather, we remain dependent on God's Word, through which the character and intent of God's activity is made clear, so we seek and recognize God there where he wishes to be sought and recognized. In this way, *sola fide* (that is, the fact that God justifies through faith alone) is also emphasized. Only those who put their trust in God and honor him can hope for something from God.

The divinity of God consists in God alone being the creator and the giver of all good things. We are in every instance dependent on God, even when our reason wishes to devise its own path to salvation. Reason argues religiously according to the notion that since God has given humans something good, they should give something to God in return. Such a reciprocal relationship between God and humanity, however, amounts to an assault against God's divinity, since humans would thereby attempt to pay God back for what he has given them:

> But that is to give his own back to God, as though it were not God's but ours. Even reason denounces as wicked and foolish the notion that someone who is generous not with his own property but with someone else's is doing anything special.[14]

Human beings can only give God something that God has first given them. But this would make no sense. As far as God is concerned, no achievement of ours matters, only our thanks. Yet even here, Luther qualifies this by pointing out that even our expression of thanks to God is not possible without God's help. Faith as trust remains the only human reaction that is appropriate in response to God.

The divinity of God is revealed in God's creation when he creates out of nothing, indeed, under the guise of the opposite. Correspondingly, faith anticipates something from God precisely where there is nothing to be seen, and faith perseveres against all adversity. Thus the divinity of God and faith correspond to one another. Faith is directed toward God alone and trusts God, from whom and to whom all things are and through whom alone justification is possible. Humans, therefore, will only act properly if they rely wholly on God. Faith is not turning off our own power of reason, nor does it call for a sacrifice of one's intellect. Instead, it is a complete reliance on God, without whom we can do nothing and to whom we are indebted for everything. Those who put their complete trust in God are not abandoned but place themselves under the protection of God, who is not only creator and sustainer but also redeemer. Yet the question remains: To what extent are humans capable of professing faith in God?

5

Humanity between God and Satan

Luther shared the vivid belief in demons and the devil that was common in the late Middle Ages. Demons lived in forest and field, swamp and moor, ponds and clouds; and witches carried out all sorts of mischief. At the Diet of Augsburg (1530), according to Luther each bishop had brought as many devils along with him "as a dog has fleas on St. John's Day."[1] But in contrast to this and similar popular opinions Luther shared, one must not forget Luther was also able to present the central themes of the Christian faith without making reference to the devil. In many of his sermons, there is no mention at all to be found of the devil. But this also has to do with the fact that in the structure of the theology of the Middle Ages, the devil occupied no fixed place. Nevertheless, the devil played a large role in Luther's perception of life. His strong sense of evil and his aversion to it come together for Luther in the figure of the devil. Luther's devil has more hellish majesty than the medieval devil, for he is more powerful and frightful and is to be taken more seriously. According to Luther, we can say three things about the devil: first, he is the adversary of God; second, he battles with God for humanity; and finally, he serves as an instrument of God.

SATAN AS GOD'S ADVERSARY

Luther speaks only occasionally about the devil's origin, his fall, and the nature of his existence. Of much more importance for Luther is the devil's reign and activity in the world. Yet Luther does believe the devil to be a creature of God equipped with consciousness, understanding, and will. Luther says that before his fall, the devil "was a very handsome angel and a decidedly outstanding creature. But . . . he was inflamed with envy, anger, and indignation against God."[2] Luther describes the devil as the powerful leader of the evil angels, whom he commands like a monarch. For Luther, therefore, the devil is not some cosmic principle but a personal being. Luther also speaks of him as the true archenemy of Christ and his kingdom, the one whom all other enemies must serve. The devil is the god of sin and death, as well as the author and distributor of both. He is called "prince of sin" and "prince of death," "potent spirit and lord of the whole world," and "his power is greater than that of ten Turkish kaisers."[3] In his hymn "A Mighty Fortress," Luther writes of the devil, "With dread craft and might he arms himself to fight. On earth he has no equal."[4] The devil rules in the world through demons, evil people, and heretics, and he has founded a kingdom of sin and disobedience from which only the power of God can rescue us. He is the embodiment of evil and can do only evil.

As the great adversary of God, the devil is seen by Luther behind everything that opposes God's ultimate will for the creation and humanity. The devil is active in misfortune, in diseases and other life crises, and in death, for he is the master and holder of power over death. He tempted the first humans to sin and remains the tempter and inciter of evil. He is at work in history against God and Christ and against truth and the gospel. The devil hates Christ and persecutes him and all those who belong to him. Therefore the devil stands behind all the enemies of God, behind the misinterpretation of Scripture, and behind all heresies and pagan philosophy. He cannot bear the pure Word of God and true doctrine, and seeks to adulterate them, especially their all-decisive content, which is justification through faith alone. The devil brings all his forces to bear in order to destroy the doctrine of justification. He makes people blind to the clear Word of God, and he causes reason to stumble over God's Word. He hardens human hearts so they do not fear the wrath of God and do not realize their true situation. He brings about human security, arrogance, and apathy, as well as the hopeless despairing of the mercy of God and Christ.

The threat posed by the devil and his seduction can be avoided by no one. The devil has a share in the dimension of the divine being, so he is omnipresent. Hence the power of God and of the devil are opposed to one another, and a great conflict ensues between them that permeates all of history and keeps it in a state of turmoil. History is, therefore, a witness to the battle of the devil against God, of God against the devil, and of the true God against the anti-god. The devil desires to be God, for the devil is the "ruler of this world" (John 12:31) and "god of this world" (2 Corinthians 4:4)[5]. He stands against God as an opponent to be taken seriously. Although his power is so great that he can be called the god of this world, the singular divinity of the true God is never for a single moment called into question. Luther limits the dualism between God and the devil through the omnipotence and sole activity of God. Nevertheless, God and the devil battle over humanity and for dominion of the earth.

GOD AND SATAN IN THE BATTLE FOR HUMANITY

Luther wrote, "Each person either lives with Christ against the devil or with the devil against Christ."[6] The world is the kingdom of the devil, and he is its lord, prince, and god. The world is subjected to his cruel tyranny, because he holds the hearts of humans captive in his bonds and afflicts them with all his power and might to force their subservience. His activity extends over body and soul. He plagues and torments the conscience and leads people astray into false doctrine, as well as into either a state of false security or into the despair of unbelief. He strikes and punishes with sickness and countless evils to destroy human beings. This affliction of humanity reaches its climax in death, over which the devil holds power as master and butcher, even though death does not have its origin or power in him but in God.

Because there is no neutral territory in human beings' relationship to God relative to their salvation or condemnation, they are always either under the power of God or of Satan. As Luther wrote in *The Bondage of the Will,*

> The human will is placed between the two like a beast of burden. If God rides it, it wills and goes where God wills. . . . If Satan rides it, it wills and goes where Satan wills. Nor can it choose to run to either of the two riders or to seek him out, but the riders themselves contend for the possession and control of it.[7]

Moreover, Satan works in human beings in a manner similar to God when he gains power over them. Both push humans along through the dynamic of their wills without rest or quiet: the devil toward evil, God along the path of good. Whoever does not belong to Christ and is not living in the power of his spirit is ruled by the devil. The devil allows no one to be snatched away from him through any power other than the Spirit of God (see Luke 11:21f.) Through Christ, God snatches human beings out of grasp of the devil.

In baptism humans are freed from the devil, because it is through baptism that they receive their portion of what Christ has accomplished on earth, namely the defeat of the devil. Yet this liberation from the devil's power can only be asserted in lifelong battle against him. Humans are confronted with an either/or situation: either fight against the devil or capitulate before him: "Choose, then, whether you prefer to wrestle with the devil or whether you prefer to belong to him. . . . If you refuse to be his, defend yourself, go at him!"[8] The weapon in this fight is the Word of God. This is true for the individual, as well as for the church as a whole, for both must offer resistance to the devil through faith and the preaching of the Word of God. Because faith is not found in everyone, the devil remains powerful in the world and in history. Christianity awaits with anticipation the final judgment, when Christ in his second coming will once and for all take away the devil's power. Yet at present, the devil works all sorts of evil on humans. He beguiles and seduces them through delusions and other means, and he brings bad weather, fired, diseases, and wars on them. Through these afflictions, he seeks to incite humans to sin, to distrust God, and to fight with one another. The devil is the great liar, who deceives humans into believing those things are good that in reality are destructive and that cause the soul to descend into fear and misery.

Luther's concept of the devil is also built on the experience that external impressions and events often set evil impulses lose in human beings and bring on them a multitude of evil, the origin of which is mysterious. In his thoughts about the devil, he expresses the sentiment that evil is a unified force that penetrates the entire natural realm of life. The all-encompassing reality of human sin is also founded on this destructive spiritual principle, which holds power over the whole realm of nature. Through his concept of the devil, Luther gives drastic expression to the terrible, superhuman power of evil in the world. Luther seeks in this way to guard humans from self-assurance, since the knowledge of this anti-godly destructive power prevents them from becoming set in their laziness and security. For Luther, the devil is thoroughly evil; he is the adversary of God who battles God for control of creation. Yet the devil is at the same time God's instrument, as are all things in the world.

THE DEVIL AS GOD'S INSTRUMENT

The brutal and frightening power of Satan is neither autonomous nor absolute. In his express rejection of a Manichean dualism between God and anti-god, Luther ultimately attributes the power and authority of the devil to God:

> Behold how wisely Moses [in Psalm 90] speaks when he attributes such wrath directly to the creator; in this way Manichaeus can't come with his great ideas and make two gods, one good and merciful, and the other evil. For Moses does not say that the devil destroys people and brings them to nothing, but rather you [God] yourself. . . . It is God's work and in the deepest sense God's wrath. . . . God indeed makes use of the devil to martyr and kill us; but because the devil is not capable of this, God willed, then, in such a way to punish sin in us.[9]

This means that God uses the devil to punish our sinfulness. Thus Luther can also say that the devil has received his power and authority from God. He embodies the wrath and justice of God, since God uses him as his tool, indeed, as his executioner, to bring his punishment on us. The hands and feet of the devil are the dreadful, atrocious claws of the wrath of God and of eternal death. The devil does not, then, rule unrestrictedly, but only so far as the wrath of God extends. His authority is derived and limited and is contingent on the ultimate authority of God against whom alone we have sinned. Only in this way can we understand how Luther is often able to set God's wrath and the devil alongside one another, and to attribute to the later what he confesses to be the work of former. With reference to Ephesians 2:3 and 2 Timothy 2:26 he says, we are "children of wrath, and . . . held captive at Satan's will," or "we are swallowed up by the devil and God's wrath."[10]

Nevertheless, it would be an oversimplification simply to view the devil as cooperating harmoniously with God in this activity of punishment. Luther also contrasts the punishment of God with the destructive power of the devil: "He [God] is a merciful God and does not punish so as to annihilate or plow us under as the devil would do, so that neither help nor counsel would remain."[11] Or, "God is not a devil; he is not a devourer or a carnivore, as you [Satan] are, . . . He is merciful to sinners, perfect and incorruptible, faithful and righteous."[12] In this way, Luther sets the devil, who terrifies, kills, and slaughters, over against God, who alone brings life and comfort.

Despite his relative independence, the devil's might is subject to the far more encompassing power of God, which punishes and judges even the devil and which leads to human salvation. Satan has power only when and where God grants him leeway, and this, contrary to outward appearances, is not without limits: "For if he had full power to rage as he pleased, you would not live for an hour."[13] The limits of satanic power are bound to the self-limitation of divine wrath based on the love of God. The devil's might, therefore, serves only the purposes of God's wrath. The devil's power extends as far as the wrath of God and is only unlimited to the extent that the wrath of God is unlimited. Yet Luther does not locate the limitation and contingency of the devil's dominion in either the wrath or power of God but rather in God's overwhelming mercy. The power of God is the force that sustains, equips, and tirelessly moves human beings and all other creatures. Through this force, the wrath of God provides the devil with the authority and space for the full development of his destructive power and yields to the devil, with sin and death as unrestricted spheres of activity.

The love of God impedes the destructive activity of Satan. While it is the devil's job to turn good into bad, the power, wisdom, and love of God are evident in that the devil, against his will, must serve the good and work toward the honor and salvation of human beings. God uses even the devil and evil angels. Their goal is to corrupt all things, but God does not allow this unless it is for well-deserved punishment of humans. God lets pestilence, war, and other problems come on human beings, so they might be humbled before him, fear him, abide by him, and call on him. The devil must then ultimately serve God through the very means by which he sought to inflict damage: "For God is the kind of Master who can use the devil's wickedness, that he might bring forth good from it."[14]

According to Luther, we see in the devil's activity that God does not act in a genuinely evil or demonic manner. God brings about good under the appearance of its evil opposite and can also make such pedagogical use of evil that the end result is good. Because God is good, he does not condone evil as such but views it rather as a means toward the punishment of sinners so their consciences are awakened to their guilt and helplessness. God works in this manner because he wills evil only as punishment, in order that the good that it opposes will stand out more clearly. Only in light of this presupposition is the following sentence of Luther's understandable: "God incites the devil to evil but God does not do evil."[15] This statement can be affirmed when one continues further with Luther: "because it pleased God so." Thus the wrath of God over sin manifests itself in the work of the devil. When God in wrath abandons humans, the devil attacks them according to the will of God and brings unbelief, despair, and death on them. God need only take his hand from us or give the devil free reign, and the punishment for sin comes upon us.

We do not, however, encounter God in fortune and some other power in misfortune, but rather *one* God who remains ever faithful and unwavering in his steadfastness—neither quick to friendliness nor quick to anger but always merciful, even when he punishes us. Although Satan is active as the instrument of God, humans are confronted with God alone. What is accomplished through God's wrath and through Satan are largely one and the same, for the devil is indeed God's devil. Yet at the same time he remains the devil, the enemy of God who seeks the opposite of all that God wills.

Yet how are the intention and activity of Satan related to the work of God, especially in connection with God's work of wrath? Luther explains this by using the example of Job. This pious man is afflicted by genuine works of the devil. Nevertheless, Scripture attributes these ultimately to God. What does this mean? "God does not do evil things but uses instrumental means."[16] Two things are thereby to be observed. First, it is God who works through his instruments. And second, in what God inflicts on people, one must distinguish between what God does and what is done by God's instruments. It is God whom we recognize to be at work in everything bad that happens to us through the means of God's instruments. Under no circumstances may we attribute misfortune or death to some separate, demonic power, for in doing so we would introduce a dualism. It is true that we must view the work of God and of Satan as one, but we must also distinguish dialectically between the two. But why make this distinction?

Luther clearly insisted that one must distinguish between the activity of God and of Satan, even though they are one and the same, because their intentions and goals are radically different. Both assail and challenge human beings to the utmost. But God does it for salvation so human beings can be freed from their own selves and all self-confidence, and flee to the arms of the merciful God. Satan, in contrast, seeks to snatch humans once and for all away from God. Christians recognize through faith that everything that happens ultimately works toward their salvation, while others who are confronted with the same negative experiences despair of their misfortune and depart from God. Tribulation, therefore, always has two faces: the face of God and the face of the devil. Although God is also the God of Satan, Satan continues to work ultimately toward the goal that human beings renounce their faith in God.

It is remarkable that in our rational world, superstitions have had such a great influence. Horoscopes, which are founded on a belief that the stars guide our fate; the belief in witches, which assumes that some people have extraordinary powers and insights; and Satan worship, with its perverse practices of animal and human sacrifice have attracted people throughout the ages. At the same time, Satan and other negative forces have fallen prey in official theology to a pervasive demythologizing, so they are either not spoken of at all or they are explained away psychologically.

One could, to be sure, claim that such negative forces are mere remnants of the Middle Ages that no longer have a place in our rational world. If they still occur today, then it might be argued that this demonstrates that those groups within society that are trying to escape the modern world feel their backs are against the wall. Their attention to these negative phenomena provides them the opportunity to express their discontent with modern civilization. The interest in these forces might also be seen as an indication that some now wish to control these forces in order to master the future, because other possibilities have not brought about the desired results. Occult practices would therefore be a further effort to control the world. Finally, experimentation with occult phenomena could be viewed as an extreme search for a thrill, similar to experimentation with drugs. In each of these efforts to explain the great interest in the occult and in the negative powers highlighted within the occult, there is certainly a measure of truth.

We must, however, concern ourselves with another, very different possibility. In the attempt to place all things under human reason, an important part of reality could have been suppressed or simply forgotten. This neglect of an aspect of reality is to be observed in the following way. Just when we thought we had achieved final mastery over the world and nature because the whole world had become comprehensible and manageable through technology and reason, precisely at this time our existence seems to be threatened as never before.

The world, which we mastered and controlled, now threatens our own existence. The world in which we live does not let itself be brought under control, any more than we are able to permanently get around the threatening and negative powers. They announce their return with vehemence.

When we admit that threatening and negative forces influence our world, does that make Luther's statements about the devil and demons more credible? In regard to this question, the following must be said:

1. The negative things that take place in the world and in the lives of individuals are of such destructive, anti-godly character that one can neither attribute them to God without making God into a demon, nor simply credit them to human beings without minimizing these events. The reality of the anti-godly, destructive powers that were self-evident for Luther is here to be acknowledged, even if Luther's anthropomorphic concept of the devil is no longer tenable today.

2. Seen from the perspective of the divinity of God, it is not justified to introduce a second power equal to God but yet with negative intentions.

3. Consequently, the anti-godly powers must be viewed as powers that, although operating destructively, are ultimately unable to impede the saving activity of God. This means that they must eventually, even if unwillingly, contribute to the glory of God.

4. What is negative in this world is always ambiguous. On the one hand, it can be enigmatically understood as the just results of our estranged existence from God, but on the other hand, as the outcome of a chaotic activity.

5. The reason God, in spite of his divinity, does not make it impossible for the negative to occur is to be found in part in the freedom God grants everyone, and in part in the mystery of God's will, which cannot be fathomed.

6

THE ORDERING ACTIVITY OF GOD
(THE TWO KINGDOMS)

The Lutheran doctrine of the two kingdoms stands within a long tradition that can be traced back to the Gospel of John, in which the evangelist speaks on the one hand of the kingdom of God (John 3:3), and on the other hand of the rulers of this world (John 12:31) and their sphere of authority. Later St. Augustine spoke of a "worldly city" and of a "city of God." Luther has often been accused of promoting a quietistic stance and silencing the church in regard to political, economic, and social problems through his doctrine of the two kingdoms. Some have even wanted to see a line running from Augustine through Luther to Adolf Hitler. As we shall see, however, this accusation does not do justice to Luther.

HISTORICAL ROOTS OF LUTHER'S DOCTRINE
AND THE TWO KINGDOMS

Luther was neither an ethicist nor a political theologian. He was a biblical theologian, keenly aware of what was happening around him, and a preacher who sought to preach the gospel. His faithfulness to the Bible and his acute sense for relevant contemporary issues led him to the doctrine of the two kingdoms. Luther was aware that, according to the testimony of the New Testament, the redemption of the world was accomplished through the advent of Christ. The path back to God was cleared for his fallen creation, and its consummation was made possible. Yet God knew that sin and death would rule in our world until the final consummation of salvation. What was revealed in the life and destiny of Jesus continued to await universal implementation. The tension between the "already" and the persisting "not yet," which was most clearly expressed by Paul, was the starting point for Luther's doctrine of the two kingdoms.

Luther stood in the tradition of the Middle Ages in which a christocratic understanding of the state was prevalent. The dominion of Christ was to be realized through human dominion. During the period of the Reformation, many leading theologians, and not only those coming out of sectarian circles, held such views. Martin Bucer (1491–1551), for instance, in his book *De regno Christi* (*On the Reign of Christ*), attempted to lay the foundations for a Christian ordering of society in England under the leadership of King Edward VI. Bucer's proposal, however, was quite utilitarian, for the proposed legislation patterned after the law of Christ for which the king was supposed to be responsible very much resembled the social and political conditions in England at the time. Luther, however, was suspicious of every christocratic approach, whether it was to be implemented by the church or the state. Already in 1518, in his *Explanations of the Ninety-five Theses*, he questioned whether it was possible for the pope to hold both a spiritual and a secular *sword*. The Bible, according to Luther, spoke only of one sword, the "sword of the Spirit" (Ephesians 6:17).[1] Luther concludes from this that a doctrine claiming two swords should be cast into hell. But Luther was not the first to reject the idea that the pope was invested with two swords or two kingdoms. This doctrine, which was popular in the Middle Ages, held that Christ had entrusted the pope as his successor with the worldly and spiritual realm, and that the pope gives the worldly realm to the emperor as a fiefdom. Already William of Ockham (ca. 1285–1349) and Marsilius of Padua (ca. 1290–1342/43) had indicated that this teaching was based on a questionable allegorical interpretation of Luke 22:38. Even in Luther's time, criticism against this doctrine had not been silenced.

In 1520, however, Luther went beyond the traditional polemic against the teaching that the pope possessed two swords. In his writing *On the Papacy in Rome*, Luther took up the question whether the authority of the pope was of divine or human character. He concluded that the pope's authority was, beyond a doubt, of a worldly and not a divine nature. But Luther was also aware that the external structure of Christendom could not be abandoned, even though this structure cannot be equated with that true Christianity, which is spiritual. Both aspects of Christianity, external structure and inner substance, must be clearly distinguished, yet dare not be separated from one another, or in one form or the other held to be absolute and definitive. They belong together, just as the soul belongs to the human body. It becomes clear here why Luther moved ultimately toward a doctrine of two kingdoms with entirely distinct structures. He was concerned about the inner spiritual life of Christianity and believed that without a genuine distinction between the secular and spiritual realms, the latter would be overwhelmed in the long run by the worldliness of medieval christocracy. In this manner, the distinction between the two kingdoms serves to make possible the proclamation of the gospel, unhindered by secular interests. On the other side, it has thwarted the attempt of enthusiasts to spiritualize the world and to erect in the present a "kingdom of God" in the world.

Because of the unique historical situation of Luther's time, he was not able to follow the two kingdoms doctrine of Augustine in the development of his argument. For Augustine, Christians were still a small group of people who were under constant threat from the all-powerful pagan state. Therefore the kingdom of the world was equated with the realm that had fallen away from God. This kingdom contains anti-godly tendencies and can sometimes even be called the city of the devil. As we see in Luther's work *Temporal Authority: To What Extent it Should be Obeyed* (1523), Luther initially largely accepted this view. Humanity must be divided into two groups: One group consists of the true believers in Christ who realize the kingdom of God under the headship of Christ. The other group has no Christians in its midst and is the kingdom of the world and of the law. The world is essentially a sinful place in which Christians suffer as a small minority. It is the enemy of God and is ruled over by secular rulers. But Luther soon abandoned the Augustinian distinction, which had become outdated. In Luther's new version, the worldly kingdom included not only the state, but everything we view today as secular, such as marriage, property, vocation, and so forth. This means that Luther could no longer apply the distinction between law and gospel to the two kingdoms without qualification. The kingdom of the world (or the secular kingdom) encompasses everything necessary for the sustenance of daily life and is understood as something good.

THE UNITY OF THE TWO WAYS GOD RULES THE WORLD

It would be wrong to equate Luther's teaching of the two kingdoms with his doctrine of a kingdom of God and a kingdom of the devil. Although Luther was absolutely convinced of the opposition that existed between God and the devil, he did not think in dualistic categories. In the New Testament, however, especially in the Gospel of John, an opposition between the kingdom of God and the kingdom of the world can be seen, in which the latter is understood as a fallen world ruled by sin, death, and the devil. When Luther, however, distinguishes between Christ's kingdom and the kingdom of the world, the kingdom of the world also attests for Luther to the ordering and sustaining will of God. This is to be seen, for example, in the ordering of nature and in political legal systems. Luther acknowledged the world as God's good creation but did not naively mistake it as a world without serious problems. In contrast to the Gospel of John or Augustine, Luther does not see the destructive work of the devil as confined to the kingdom of the world or to the secular realm. The battle lines are now drawn through both kingdoms, and Satan seeks to transform them both into God-opposing chaos. Luther confesses, "Against this rule of God, however, Satan rages; for his sole purpose is to crush and destroy everything God creates and does through his rule."[2] It is God's will that both kingdoms or means of governing serve as a bulwark against the destructive attacks of the devil. This points also to the inner unity of the two kingdoms, as Luther wrote,

> God has established two kinds of government among humanity. The one is spiritual; it has no sword, but it has the Word, by means of which people are to become good and righteous, so that with this righteousness they may attain eternal life. God administers this righteousness through the Word, which he has committed to the preachers. The other kind is worldly government, which works through the sword so that those who do not want to be good and righteous to eternal life may be forced to become good and righteous in the eyes of the world. God administers this righteousness through the sword. And although God will not reward this kind of righteousness with eternal life, nonetheless, God still wishes peace to be maintained among people and rewards them with temporal blessings.[3]

This quotation from 1526 clearly shows that the same God stands behind both kingdoms and is active and present in different ways within both. Since God is active in both kingdoms according to his goodness and love, Luther concludes that God bestows a twofold blessing on humans: a material blessing for this life and a spiritual blessing for the life eternal. We can see, therefore, an expression of God's love in the unity that exists between the two kingdoms.

This unity, however, is not only to be understood theocentrically. Luther also says God has "three outward rules and in addition three outward ways or means for his own divine rule."[4] Elsewhere he wrote, "God has therefore established three hierarchies against the devil: the family, the political order, and the church."[5] Although God's lordship ultimately ties the two kingdoms together, the unity is also visible in human activity, since humans live simultaneously in both kingdoms and in all three hierarchies. As coworkers with God, humans encounter both forms of God's government, namely, God's *law* (as it comes to expression in the political realm, the family, and ecclesial structures) and God's *gospel*, as it is proclaimed to them in the preached word.

DISTINCTION AND MUTUAL PERMEATION OF THE TWO KINGDOMS

Although Luther was convinced of the fundamental unity of the two kingdoms, he never tired of emphasizing that we must distinguish properly between them. The spiritual and worldly kingdoms must be distinguished clearly as heaven and earth. The one is concerned with faith and eternal salvation, the other with external peace and the prevention of evil. The secular kingdom serves the earthly life and is finite, while the spiritual kingdom is related to life eternal, which is the ultimate goal of God's activity.

The worldly kingdom is ostensibly subordinated to the spiritual kingdom. God rules in the secular realm with his left hand, while reigning over the spiritual kingdom with his right hand. This is God's actual work, and God cannot allow anyone else to reign over souls. Christians are indeed aliens in the kingdom of the world, for they are guided by faith. Yet those who are not Christians cannot be guided by faith and love. They belong to the kingdom of the world and are instructed in proper conduct by earthly rules. Because Christians are already leading their lives as the *sword*, that is, as the worldly order requires, keeping laws within the secular realm poses no difficulty for them.

Luther correctly observed that Christians cannot escape from the kingdom of the world because we "are all caught within it, indeed, born into it, before we become Christians. Therefore, we must also remain within it so long as we live on the earth, but according to the external bodily life and existence."[6] According to our worldly needs, we are citizens of the kingdom of the world, but according to our spiritual existence, we are citizens of the spiritual kingdom. This demonstrates that despite all their differences, a mutual permeation of the two kingdoms exists.

Luther especially emphasizes one point at which our dependence on the kingdom of the world is manifest when he says that the spiritual kingdom requires peace and order in the world, in order that the Word and sacraments can be properly administered. Christians cannot lead a sheltered existence and escape the world. This dependence is further made clear in the encompassing character of the worldly kingdom, which encompasses not only human authority, government, and the orders of nature, but also marriage, family, property, business, and different vocations. These various human undertakings are carried out according to the law, or according to the sword, which for Luther are synonymous.

But how can one know the law of God if one is not even a Christian? Luther himself admits realistically that already "since the beginning of the world a wise prince is a mighty rare bird, and an upright prince even rarer."[7] Luther even writes that princes, for the most part, have been the greatest fools and the worst scoundrels. How, then, can they know the law of God? Here we must once again recall the great trust Luther placed in the natural reason God has given to all people. The kingdom of the world is ruled through reason, and political and economic decisions are not made according to the Bible but according to reason. Luther observes that Christ never preached about economic issues but left this field to human reason, so it could instruct us as to how goods should be divided and trade conducted.[8] Luther's understanding of reason, however, does not correspond to the Enlightenment conception which understood reason as the autonomous possession of humans. For Luther, even natural reason is a gift of God.

The function of reason in Luther's doctrine of the two kingdoms is clarified for us when we turn to the distinction between general and special revelation. It is obvious for Luther that God has revealed certain things to all people through general revelation, while other things are only accessible through the special revelation in Jesus Christ. The regulations and laws of this world are not given through Christ, but instead are already available through the natural law, which is a source of general revelation. Luther is, however, aware that in this world the knowledge of the will of God, which is made possible through general revelation, is often distorted and obscured as a result of human sinfulness. Yet he is convinced that it is not Christ but rather the laws of each particular nation that answer the social and cultural questions concerning what a parent, teacher, politician, or judge should do in certain situations.[9] Of course these laws are historically conditioned and have undergone many revisions. Luther challenges us, therefore, to use our reason to investigate whether these historically evolved laws still constitute an adequate expression of the natural law they are supposed to represent. Luther does not equate the natural law with the laws of a particular nation. The natural law is, moreover, the fountain from which the other laws flow and the basis on which they are to be criticized and interpreted. Yet we normally encounter the natural law in the form of a positive law, which we find in the laws and usages of a particular nation. Although Luther distinguished between the positive law of a given nation and the natural law, he sometimes identified the two—an identification that, in light of human sinfulness, is not without problems.

CHRISTIAN EXISTENCE IN THE
KINGDOM OF THE WORLD

Luther consistently maintained that Christians could also be responsible citizens. Although Christians should not exercise any secular authority among themselves, they must make use of this authority in order to preserve the peace for others. For themselves, however, they should simply obey those who exercise worldly power, thus submitting themselves to secular laws. Luther also believed that Christians should not oppose evil if this opposition benefitted only themselves. When Christians, however, occupy a secular position, as for example parent, teacher, politician, judge, and so forth, they must oppose evil to the extent that this opposition is a function of their office. Otherwise, they would neglect their responsibilities and in the long run endanger others. We have the responsibility to enforce the rules connected with our positions with the necessary resolution, yet in love. For example, I must help the neighbor who is in difficulty, and when I am a judge and anyone has injured him or her, I must punish that person to the full extent of the law. But even as a lawbreaker, the person who injured my neighbor remains my brother or sister. Evildoers must indeed be punished and their crimes condemned, but the punishment must be executed with compassion. This means that I must distribute punishment only in my role as judge and not as a private individual. I enforce the law out of my responsibility toward God's own order, not because I hate the lawbreaker.

The validity of the law is not limited to the kingdom of the world but also has its appropriate place within the spiritual kingdom, yet only as a function of an office in which the law represents God and his order. The law should never be used as a means toward personal revenge, because it must ultimately be an act of love toward one's neighbor. Luther can therefore encourage Christians to seek a secular office. If politicians and judges are necessary and one believes oneself to be qualified to fill one of these positions, then one should strive to achieve this office, otherwise the necessary authority of the office would be held in contempt and weakened. Although Luther counsels against using force either too freely or too sparingly, he admits, "To err in this direction . . . and punish too little is more tolerable, for it is always better to let a scoundrel live than to put a godly man to death."[10] Just how far Luther is from the idea of a power-hungry secular order can be seen in his advice that Christians who hold secular office should imitate Christ. Just as Christ as supreme prince came and served us without seeking to increase his own power and honor, Christians in their offices should also not strive for their own advantage but should serve those placed under their authority, protecting and defending them.

Luther's attitude toward property serves as a good example of his understanding of the service-oriented character of Christians. Luther maintained that all property, with the exception of what is needed for personal use, is unjustly possessed and has actually been stolen from God, and therefore should be used to help others. God demands of us to give generously to others.[11] Maintaining possessions becomes theft when we do not use all resources that go beyond our personal needs to alleviate the suffering of others. Luther, therefore, criticized business people who took interest from hard-working laborers. Without the slightest investment of their own and without concern for others, they profit from ambitious, hardworking men and women who are exposed to a variety of dangers in their work. To alleviate this injustice, Luther proposes that those who finance a loan receive no set annual amount of interest but rather a percentage of the profits earned by the one who took out the loan. If the profits are high, then both will fare well. But when they are low, then both will suffer. In this way, those who lend money can exhibit a genuine interest in whom they have made a loan and in their work. Here again, Lu on the service-oriented nature of secular structures is seen. T should serve people and not the free-reigning power of capital.

This view of Luther's is expressed with particular clarity when he describes the principles according to which Christian rulers should exercise their office.[12] They must in the first place turn to God with good faith and deep prayer. Then they must handle those under their authority out of love and an attitude of Christian service. Third, they must treat their advisers with a spirit of openness and nonpartisan opinion. And finally, they should confront evildoers with responsible force and severity. These arguments show that although one cannot serve both God and *mammon* (or wealth), one can serve both God and emperor. It even appears that one can better serve the emperor in the secular realm if one also serves God in the spiritual realm. Yet one might rightly inquire to what extent Luther's position goes beyond a simple advocacy of the status quo and strives for a transformation toward a more just society.

Critique of the doctrine of the two kingdoms.

Critics of Luther have said that the doctrine of the two kingdoms supports the status quo and hardly allows for any creative innovation. Of course, Luther's doctrine of two kingdoms should not be uncritically applied to our own time, just as Augustine's concept of a city of the world and a city of God could not be applied to the medieval situation without decisive modifications. The modern form of societal structure in which the authority to govern comes from the people was unknown to Luther. His emphasis on the sword and punishment through rulers might, therefore, be seen as outdated today. In the Western world, public order can only be maintained through a basic consent which must, however, be oriented toward specific values and objectives. In this regard, Luther's insistence on order, justice, and mutual concern is certainly of continuing value.

It is precisely the ordering function of authorities, however, that has been viewed with much skepticism in light of the unjust rule in the Third Reich and in formerly communist East Germany, which existed in the heartland of the Reformation. Was not Luther's doctrine of two kingdoms partly responsible for the rise of the Third Reich? In response to this question, it must first of all be noted that Adolf Hitler's first denominational support came from Catholicism. Further, one must point out that the Lutheran nations of Scandinavia, albeit with little success, sought to offer resistance to the Nazi occupation. Indeed, so many factors came into play with the rise of the Third Reich that one cannot simply lay the blame directly on the Lutherans. Also, one must understand Luther's argumentation historically. Against the medieval feudal system and its spread of terror Luther stressed the king's peace and its preservation through every available means. One cannot speak of a pure pacifism or a quietistic inaction in regard to Luther.

A second area of criticism against the Lutheran doctrine of the two kingdoms is that it contradicts the New Testament understanding of the kingdom of God. For this reason, one is particularly inclined in Reformed circles to replace the two-kingdom view with the reign of Christ in the one kingdom. Although such terminology can make very good sense, inasmuch as it is oriented to the New Testament Gospels, it must not be forgotten that in this world, true believers, nominal believers, and unbelievers live together. Christians and non-Christians live with one another in the same world. Christians do not yet enjoy an eschatological community of believers, even if the New Testament understanding of the kingdom of God presents this as having already been inaugurated. If one does not wish to make the church into a duplicate of the world, or vice versa, to place society under the explicit reign of Christ, then one must distinguish between that realm of society that allows itself expressly to be governed by the Word of God, and all other areas in which God is not even talked about and that must therefore be governed by God indirectly.

POSITIVE EVALUATIONS

Despite all the criticisms, three aspects of Luther's doctrine of the two kingdoms remain especially important for us today:

1. *The world is not only a place of sin and evil, but it also stands under the rule of God.* To simply write off the world as bad not only goes against the prevailing sentiment of most people but also contradicts the Bible. The description of the earth as a vale of trouble, labor, and tears, and as the domain of the devil from which Christians will soon be delivered when they reach heaven, represents only one aspect of the biblical truth. If one sets up this partial truth as absolute, one gets the impression that the gospel cannot say anything positive about the world. Yet it is the understanding of the Old as well as the New Testament that God cares for this fallen world, protecting and preserving it. Luther's emphasis on the reign of God within the secular realm reminds us that the world, even in its God-alienated state, is not without God. God's presence in his disclosure in Jesus Christ is merely the special way that leads to eternal salvation, in which God is with his creation. If we reject the notion of a general revelation, which in hidden and faint ways always expresses itself in specific situations, we would deny the divinity of God. The result would be an

unbiblical, dualistic worldview in which the world would exist without God. However, the persistent religiosity of humans by which religious themes continue to occupy our attention, despite all the secularization of the day-to-day world, would be difficult to explain apart from a general revelation.

2. *If we do not want to perish with the world, then it must be a place of mutual cooperation and concern.* The natural law, which Luther correctly saw expressed in the golden rule, is fundamental for the survival of a society. If the golden rule as the fundamental principle of community life is denied (for instance, in the family, in a people, or in the whole of humanity), then human relationships will suffer in the long run. This can be recognized in the state capitalism of former socialist nations, as well as in Western-style individualistic capitalism. Both forms of life together show too little mutual consideration and concern for fellow human beings. In both cases, society is not able to bear the long-term results. The increasingly obvious Northern-Southern Hemisphere conflict on our globe functions in a similarly disturbing fashion. One can even demonstrate that humans ultimately destroy themselves if they do not exhibit sufficient care of creation as a gift of God, but rather only selfishly exploit its resources. The natural law functions as regulator, so we might recognize our own exploitative tendencies toward other people and toward nature and correspondingly correct these. Because humans are blessed with reason, there is also cause for optimism that we will not permanently destroy the God-given environment in which we live, but rather live peacefully with one another on the earth. Yet in our striving for mutual concern, we should realistically remember that the earth is only God's worldly realm, and that dreams of heaven on earth are utopian and unjustified.

3. *Power always brings with it a demonic temptation toward its misuse.* In contrast to many great religious figures before and after him, Luther was very much aware of this temptation. When Luther chided evil leaders and held their abuses before them, he knew humans were, by their sinful nature, centered on themselves; they are beings estranged from God. For this reason, Luther often turned to Christian leaders and encouraged Christians in general to seek public office. Although Christians know the natural law and are willing to obey it, they are not guided by its often hazy precepts. They live according to the example of Christ and by his grace. Therefore they can establish signs and pointers to God's will in a demonic world. As the community of the body of Christ, their aim is to proleptically actualize the future provided by Christ. They need not despair because they are only a minority or because no one seems to take notice of their efforts. They can and must announce the future Christ has provided, because they know the one who was the first to live as God intended humans to live.

Therefore, both symbolically and literally they should represent mutuality in their communal structures. Christ overcame the inner contradictions of humanity by dying the death of this world and beginning a new life. Yet Christians can at present realize this new life only in a fragmentary fashion. They actively and with anticipation await with the whole creation the universal coming of the new creation and the final redemptive act of God. At this future point, the two forms of God's administration will be fused into God's one world. In the contemporary world, however, we continue to live within two distinct kingdoms.

Luther always had a healthy mistrust of authority. In contrast to the Anabaptists, he did not close himself off from the world but instead called for Christian engagement with the world. His criticisms of the sociopolitical relationships of his time were not destructive and did not reflect a mistrust of the ruling powers as such, but he was always conscious of his responsibility toward the entire community. He followed no particular party line. During the Peasant War, for example, he initially took up the complaints of the peasants (who were being exploited by the nobility and upper classes) and warned the ruling class, "For rulers are not appointed to exploit their subjects for their own profit and advantage, but to be concerned about the welfare of their subjects."[13] Yet he also warned the peasants, "The fact that the rulers are wicked and unjust does not excuse disorder and rebellion, for the punishing of wickedness is not the responsibility of everyone, but of the worldly rulers who bear the sword."[14] He warned both sides: "For God's sake, . . . take hold of these matters properly, with justice and not with force or violence, and do not start endless bloodshed."[15] However, when the peasants took up arms, Luther reminded the princes of their duty, "for in this case a prince and lord must remember that according to Romans 13[:4], he is God's minister and the servant of his wrath, and the sword has been given to him against such people."[16] Christians, whether in a ruling position or as ordinary citizens, must therefore always look to what is right, and take the side of what is right, and seek without resorting to violence to help what is right to gain the victory, using all means at their disposal, so that the well-being of the entire community will be promoted.

In many of Luther's letters, he took a stance regarding the political issues of his day. In so doing, he did not seek to become involved in political life by virtue of his reputation. Rather, he saw it as his Christian duty not to let the political events of the day pass by without comment. Luther almost always rejected advising anyone to resist the powers that be, although as evidenced by his very clear criticisms, neither did he seek to shelter them. If the governing authority is influenced by speaking the truth to it, Luther writes, "well and good; if not, you are excused, you suffer wrong for God's sake."[17] We owe the

governing authorities the word of truth, whether that be criticism or affirma-
tion, even though we should not count on its being accepted. Luther was
convinced that an irresponsible governing authority would not go unpunished,
for God overthrows the powerful from their thrones and is able "to eradicate
their roots, along with their name and the memory of them."[18] God himself
reigns and will in his own good time abolish an insubordinate government.

Luther feared that those in the Roman church who rejected his reforms
might brand him a leader of rebellion. This fear played a role in his disapprov-
ing attitude toward opposing authority. He feared that under the pretext of
putting down what they would label as "Luther's rebellion," the political authorities could roll back the reforms he had set in motion. In order not to give them
any excuse to go on the offensive, Luther was very concerned to maintain order.
For this reason, it was also very difficult for those influenced by Luther—such
as Hans von Donanyi, Carl Friedrich von Goerdeler, and General Ludwig Beck,
who took part in the July 20, 1944, attempt to overthrow Hitler—to finally
make the transition to an active revolt. Following the thought of Luther, they
understood Romans 13 ("Whoever resists authority resists what God has
appointed, and those who resist will incur judgment") as a warning against
every self-proclaimed uprising against authority. They asked themselves, therefore, whether Hitler could still be considered the legitimate authority.

After the war, there appeared an important book on political ethics by the
Lutheran theologian Walther Künneth (*Politik zwischen Dämon und Gott*
[Berlin: Lutherisches Verlagshaus, 1954]), in which he portrayed politics as existing in tension between Romans 13 (authority as the ordering power of God)
and Revelation 13 (the demonic state), and conceded the right to rebel against
the state under certain, carefully considered conditions. One should not, therefore, rise up against anything and everything in the opinion that, as a Christian,
one knows better than others what is best for the general good. Luther himself
had a healthy mistrust of attempts to Christianize the world:

> If anyone attempted to rule the world by the gospel and to abolish all tempo-
> ral law and sword on the plea that all are baptized and Christian, and that,
> according to the gospel, there shall be among them no law or sword—or need
> for either—pray tell me, friend, what would he be doing? He would be loos-
> ing the ropes and chains of the savage wild beasts and letting them bite and
> mangle everyone, meanwhile insisting that they were harmless, tame, and gen-
> tle creatures; but I would have the proof in my wounds. Just so would the
> wicked under the name of Christian abuse evangelical freedom, carry on their
> rascality, and insist that they were Christians subject neither to law nor sword.[19]

Because there are sinful people in this world, one cannot dispense with a political order that judges according to the principles of justice. But such systems need the cooperation and engagement of Christians who should further the principle of justice and oppose injustice.

7

SCRIPTURE ALONE

Luther was a biblical theologian. Scripture alone (*sola scriptura*), therefore, became the basic premise of Lutheran theology. Bible translation and the broad availability of Bibles were of great significance for the spread of Luther's teaching. Johannes Gutenberg (1394/1399–1468) had revolutionized the production of books by using reusable metal letters in a printing press. It fell to Luther to revolutionize Bible translation. He worked from the original languages, rendering the Old Testament from Hebrew and the New Testament from Greek. First, he had to acquire adequate knowledge of both languages. This task was made more difficult because, at the time of Luther, the study of Greek and Hebrew in the German universities was still in its early stages, and reliable lexicons and grammars were rare. Luther therefore had to rely on the counsel of well-informed friends and experts. For the first translation of the New Testament, the so-called September Bible of 1522, Luther frequently relied on reformer Philipp Melanchthon's knowledge of the Greek language. With the Old Testament, Luther turned for advice to the Jews, who were particularly helpful to him in his translation of Old Testament laws into German. The Wittenberg Hebrew scholar Matthäus Aurogallus (ca. 1490–1543) also assisted him. To the very end of his life, Luther worked on his translation of the Bible, so later editions contained many improvements.

Many scholars before Luther had translated the Bible into German. Each of them depended on the Latin translation of the Bible known as the *Vulgate*. Yet hardly any of these translations found their way into the hands of the people because, according to the official opinion of the church, the Word of God did not belong in the hands of lay people. These translations were also difficult to understand because they often followed too rigidly the structure of the Latin on which they were based. Martin Luther was the first to insist that one must "look the people in the face," that is to say, one must bring the biblical texts to the people. To this end, Luther used the diplomatic language of the Saxon court, which was largely familiar to both the middle and the high Germans. Although Luther was especially careful to render the objective meaning of the biblical text in unabbreviated form into German, he also succeeded through his choice of words in conforming the text to contemporary thought and language patterns. Luther's translation of the Bible was an important linguistic work of art that was even praised by his opponents. He reported in a table talk, "I have this testimony from Duke George, that he once said, If only the monk would put the whole Bible into German and then go to the place where he belongs!"[1] (Duke George of Saxony, who clung to the old faith, was an irreconcilable opponent of Luther. But even he wished that Luther would complete his translation of the Bible.)

As soon as Luther's translation appeared, it became an absolute best-seller. Between 1522, when the September Bible appeared, and 1546, the year of Luther's death, more than 300 full or partial editions of the Bible were published. Even assuming that each printing ran to only 2,000 copies, then altogether there were probably at least 750,000 copies of Luther's translation of the Bible sold during his lifetime. This incredible number of Bibles is all the more astounding when we consider that the price for Luther's translation of the Bible, as for all books at that time, was very high. For the translation of the New Testament published in 1522, the price was between one-half and one and one-half guldens, a price that, compared with the average yearly wage of a domestic maid at one and one-half guldens, would be considered very expensive even in our time. Luther, however, did not receive a single cent for his Bible translation. The profit went entirely into the coffers of the publishers.

For Luther, the translation of the Bible was indispensable, for the Word of God and Scripture belong together. The Word is only found in Scripture and must always be measured by it. Because we are each responsible for our own faith, we cannot rely on other people's interpretation of Scripture and believe on the basis of their authority. Rather, every Christian depends on Scripture but must first be familiar with it. Although Luther emphasized different biblical writings in view of their varying theological content and weight, the Scripture as a whole had only one content for Luther, which was Jesus Christ.

CHRIST AS THE SOLE CONTENT OF SCRIPTURE

Christ is the Word of God become human. It is for this reason that the Bible can be the Word of God only when its single and entire content is Christ. To be sure, Luther knew that the Bible contained more than words from and about Jesus. It also included the Old Testament law that, according to Luther, pointed to Christ, who is freed from the law and is the content of the gospel. Therefore, either directly or indirectly, Christ is the content of Scripture. Luther was aware that the biblical canon was formed within the church over a period of time. This, however, does not allow the church to place itself above Scripture, for the contents of Scripture are authenticated by Christ and not by the church. As the content of Scripture, Christ himself attests to the truth of Scripture. Just as John the Baptist did not stand over Christ, so also according to Luther, the church cannot rule or stand over Scripture. No human institution can authorize Scripture, that is, lend it credibility. It bears its authority within itself through that which speaks from within it, namely Jesus Christ. Only to the extent that the church places itself under Scripture and satisfies its requirements can the church itself be authorized by Scripture: "The gospel is not believed because the church confirms it, but rather because people sense that it is the Word of God."[2] The self-attestation of Scripture corresponds to its self-interpretation.

Martin Luther rejected the fourfold interpretation of Scripture common at his time and stressed that Scripture should always be interpreted *literally*. It should not be translated *allegorically*, that is, in the sense of the church and its teachings; nor *tropologically*, meaning as related to ethics and morals; nor *anagogically*, as pointing to the eschatological fulfillment. Scripture must in the first place be understood literally, in the sense that its original authors meant it. Because this sense comes to the fore nowhere so directly and vitally as in Scripture itself, this means that Scripture must interpret its own self. Luther pleaded, therefore, for an interpretation that originates from Scripture and is not imposed on it. If another authority would interpret Scripture, this authority would authenticate Scripture, and the character of Scripture as final authority would be lost: "Scripture, therefore, is its own light. It is good, then, when Scripture interprets itself."[3]

The principle of Scripture's self-interpretation is, on the one hand, directed toward Rome, where it was argued that only the teaching office of the church is able authoritatively to interpret Scripture. On the other hand, Luther also used this principle against the enthusiasts, who contended that a special gift of the Spirit enabled them to correctly understand Scripture. Luther, nevertheless, suggests that only people who are moved by God's Spirit can interpret Scripture. Yet the Spirit comes to them alone through the Scriptures. If we expect such a spiritual gift through institutions and events outside the Scripture, then we elevate these above Scripture and ultimately interpret Scripture according to our own wishes. For Luther, this ultimately means that Scripture should always be interpreted according to its literal sense. One should make exception to this principle only when the text itself forces one to adopt a figurative understanding. If Scripture, on the contrary, is interpreted "spiritually," then everyone can impose his or her own spirit on the words, and Scripture loses its clarity.

The self-interpretation of Scripture, however, presupposes that Scripture is in itself clear and understandable. Luther was firm in this belief, especially in view of the Roman church's teaching that Scripture is unclear and can be rightly interpreted only by the teaching office of the church. The clarity of Scripture is seen already by Luther in the fact that Jesus and the apostles referred to

Scripture, that is, what we now call the Old Testament, in their teaching, and in doing so testify to the general clarity of Scripture. For Luther, it is not a dogmatic postulate that Scripture is clear and understandable. This recognition was reaffirmed through Luther's own study of the Bible. The fact that many people either do not understand Scripture or understand it incorrectly was explained by Luther by indicating that these people were either held captive by Satan or, in the case of the pious, that God allowed them to continue in error for a certain time to show them that only he could enlighten them.

The interpretation of Scripture must always occur from its center, that is, from Christ. Of course, the ruling scholastic theology of the time also knew that Christ was the center of Scripture. Yet Christ was usually understood morally as a law-oriented teacher of virtues, as we see in Erasmus or the legal-minded reformers of the late Middle Ages. For Luther, however, Christ as the center of Scripture is synonymous with the free grace of God, on whom alone human salvation depends. Luther's view of Christ comes primarily form the New Testament proclamation, especially from the writings of Paul and the Gospel of John. But Luther also found testimony to Christ already in the Old Testament:

> Therefore, what is preached about Christ is all one Gospel, although every writer has his own distinctive literary style. . . . But whenever it deals with Christ as our Savior and states that we are justified and saved through faith in him without our works, then there is one Word and one Gospel.[4]

The christocentric exposition of Scripture is an interpretation of the biblical message derived from the gospel of justification through faith alone. In the event that a passage of Scripture contradicts the gospel and stands in opposition to the rest of Scripture seen as a whole, then this passage has no authority as the Word of God. This was applied by Luther, for example, in the case of the Letter of James. Luther declared that one must interpret this letter according to the rest of Scripture and must not derive any theological propositions from it that would oppose the plain and clear direction of Scripture as a whole. If this method of interpretation is not followed, then one would have to reject James as unbiblical. Hence Luther's principle of the gospel-centered exposition of Scripture also becomes biblical criticism when the text does not appropriately represent the gospel.

LIMITS OF BIBLICAL CRITICISM

Luther occasionally criticized the biblical documents when he pointed to contradictions and discrepancies within them. Nevertheless, it would be inaccurate to view him as one of the founders of historical biblical criticism, because he made such critical observations only very occasionally and did not give any great weight to them. Essential for Luther was that we have the right understanding of Scripture and the right articles of faith, that is, the hermeneutic key to understand the Bible. Questions of historical criticism were, in contrast, secondary for him. Even when Luther theologically criticized certain parts of the canon, the standard he judged them against was either Christ or the gospel of free grace and justification through faith alone. One could also say that for Luther what was apostolic was decisive. That meant for him, by way of content, that Christ as Savior must be proclaimed loud and clear: "It is the office of a true apostle to preach of the passion and resurrection and office of Christ."[5]

The apostolic character of a New Testament author is witnessed to in the contents of his writing, namely in the clarity of his testimony of Christ. This is the standard Luther used to classify a book as canonical: "All the genuine sacred books agree in this, that all of them preach and inculcate Christ."[6] If this characteristic is deficient or entirely missing in one of the canonical writings, then its author cannot be an apostle. By applying this criterion, Luther determined in his "Preface to the New Testament" in 1522 which books are the truest and noblest in the New Testament. They are the Gospel of John and the First Letter of John, the letters of Paul (especially the letters to the Romans, Galatians, and Ephesians), as well as the First Letter of Peter.[7] Although the Gospel of John reports only a few miracles, it is truly the chief of the four Gospels and is far ahead of the others. Although the others report many miracles, they do not proclaim the gospel as clearly as John. Luther recognized the intention of the Letter of James, that it is directed against those who would put their trust in faith without works. Yet he argues that the letter was not fully up to this task. In regard to the letter to the Hebrews Luther points out the great difference in its content compared to the other apostolic writings, yet he has a great appreciation for it precisely because of its witness to the priestly office of Christ and its interpretation of the Old Testament.

Also in 1522 Luther wrote concerning the Revelation of John that he could sense no inspiration of the Holy Spirit in this book. Hence he placed it at the end of the Bible together with the Letter of Jude. In 1530 Luther wrote a new critical preface to the book of Revelation in which he interpreted the book in relation to the history of the church and in this way highlighted its continuing value to the church.[8] But he was still not able to recognize it as one of the chief books of the Bible.

Luther's assessments of individual books of the New Testament are significant because, if for no other reason, they show he applied criticism to the canon and did not understand the Bible and all of its parts as a book of laws all having the same weight. He pointed to differences within the canon in terms of whether a book stood nearer or further from the center of Scripture. He also indicated varying degrees of evangelical clarity and thereby varying degrees of authority and significance for the church. Hence for Luther there existed a canon within the canon. He did not, however, express any criticisms in the name of reason by claiming, for instance, that one could no longer accept certain views of Scripture in light of a particular scientific world view or on the basis of some modern philosophy. Only in those places where he detected a clouding of the proclamation of the gospel did he question the character of a writing or a text as the Word of God. Decisive for Luther is what empowers Christianity and not what does or does not make sense to reason. Luther's biblical criticism is kept within clear boundaries and is pre-Enlightenment.

RELATIONSHIP BETWEEN THE TWO TESTAMENTS

It is important to Luther, in regard to the Word of God, to distinguish between law and gospel. This distinction, however, is not identical to that between the Old and New Testaments. In the Old Testament there is gospel, namely in the promises, just as there is also law to be found in the New Testament, as in the Sermon on the Mount. Nevertheless, the Old Testament is primarily law, while gospel dominates the New Testament. The Old Testament mainly teaches about the law and sin, whereas the New Testament brings the good news of grace and peace through the forgiveness of sins. Both Testaments are related to one another in the same way as are promise and fulfillment, because the Old Testament points toward Christ and salvation, while the New Testament testifies to these promises as fulfilled.

The entire truth of the New Testament is already hidden within the Old Testament, so it must only be opened up and revealed. Thus Luther can say,

> Everything the apostles have taught and written they have derived from the Old Testament, for everything that would take place in the future in Christ and would be preached has been proclaimed in it. . . . For this reason, they based all their preaching on the Old Testament, and there is no word in the New Testament for which one does not see behind it the Old Testament in which it was previously proclaimed.[9]

As a witness to the resurrection of the dead, Christ unveils the meaning of the first law, that God is a God of the living and not of the dead. Luther is even able to contend that the New Testament has no other function than to open up the Old Testament and to reveal the gospel hidden within it. New Testament proclamation is by its very nature Old Testament interpretation. Luther took notice of the fact that Jesus wrote nothing at all and the apostles wrote only very little, for they referred to and grounded themselves on existing writings, namely the Old Testament. The Old Testament, then, according to Luther, becomes the swaddling clothes and crib "in which Christ lies."[10] This is also the testimony of the angel to the shepherds in the nativity story. The New Testament is entirely founded on the Old Testament, even though the Old Testament is only first unveiled in the New Testament and can only be understood through it. To the extent the Old Testament bears the gospel within it and has to do with Christ, it points beyond itself, to the New Testament.

Binding nature of the Old Testament.

The Old Testament, in the form in which we have it today, is first of all the testament that God gave to Israel. The law contained within it is likewise applicable only for Israel. Hence Luther can say that the Old Testament is "the *Sachsenspiegel* of the Jews, that is to say, their law book."[11] As such, it is not directed toward Christians and is not binding for them. Luther distances himself from the enthusiasts and Anabaptists, who often turned to Old Testament regulations to justify their actions, and in doing so continued to regard the law of Moses as the binding Word of God for them. Luther responded to this view, saying, "One must not only consider whether it is the Word of God, whether God has said it, but much more, to whom he has said it, whether it applies to you."[12] In the law, God has spoken first of all to Israel and not to Christians: "For Moses is given to the Jewish people alone, and does not concern us Gentiles and Christians."[13] This applies not just to the Mosaic ceremonial law and legal code but also to the Decalogue.

The Decalogue, or Ten Commandments, is the source and center of all the laws of Israel. Even the ceremonial law and legal codes depend on it. Christ, however, is the end of the law. The ban against images (Exodus 20:4) and the Sabbath laws (Exodus 20:8) are therefore abolished. Nevertheless, the Old Testament law and the law of Moses do not remain exclusively related to Israel. It is also a special form of natural law written in the hearts of all people. To the extent that the Mosaic law and this natural law correspond, it is also applicable to non-Jews. It is not binding for them as the law of Moses, but rather obligates them through its content in their hearts and consciences. Moses is not the author but only the interpreter of the laws that are written in the hearts of all people.

When Christians teach the Mosaic law, particularly the Ten Commandments, it is because "the natural laws were never so orderly and well written as by Moses."[14] We must not, however, according to Luther, accept the Decalogue in its historical form without reflection, but must clearly distinguish between what is binding and what is not binding within it. The fear of God, for instance, remains binding, for as Luther says, God should be "feared, loved and trusted above all things." The Sabbath ban, on the other hand, as Luther's reformulation of the third law shows, is declared to be no longer applicable. It loses the status of binding, but continues to be recognized as an example in the form of "you shall keep holy the day of rest."

In the law of Moses, there are also many other regulations that can serve as examples to other peoples without being binding. As examples of these, Luther mentions the Tenth Commandment, the jubilee year, the sabbath year, and the law on divorce. He would have been pleased if these and other ordinances of the Mosaic law would have been taken over by secular law, not by compulsion (as if they were divine laws) but freely, based upon the reasonable insight that these regulations are simply exemplary. Luther was of the opinion that throughout history a people would frequently adopt laws from another people when they recognized that these laws were good. Thus, the law of the Old Testament has a continuing relevance for non-Jews. Luther also admits that the history of Israel, as we find it in the Old Testament, has a certain relevance for us. We can learn from its example how people either obeyed the law of God or were disobedient, and how God responded either with grace or wrath. Even Christians can learn from such examples, because human nature has remained the same throughout the ages. Christians, in their own individual histories with God, will continually be confronted with similar questions and decisions. The history of the people of Israel, therefore, has an exemplary significance for all people.

Christ and the Old Testament.

According to Luther, the Old Testament is a book that testifies of Christ. As law, it points to Christ and is filled with him, inasmuch as it promises and points proleptically to Christ and his church. Moses taught the law so that the people would recognize their reluctance toward the law and would strive toward grace. With these observations Luther took up the interpretation of the law as the taskmaster that leads us to Christ (Galatians 3:24f.). Similar to Moses, the prophets also point beyond themselves. Luther interprets them as both proclaimers of the promise and advocates of the law. They demonstrate how God has a very firm and strict manner confirmed in his command. The proclamation of the prophets, therefore, is to be understood christocentrically.

The Old Testament, however, does not simply lead us to Christ, for Christ is already present within it. In his actions and promises, he is already present in the God of the Old Testament. In the Old Testament we do not encounter some abstract God, but rather God the Father, who lets himself be found in certain places and under certain signs, and who gives the people his promises. These promises all point to Christ, whereby one must distinguish between the immediate promise of Christ and the anticipation of Christ. First of all, Christ is promised in the Prophets, Psalms, and the well-known messianic passages of the historical books. Even if the prophets often erred in the predictions of future historical events, which Luther concedes, they were nonetheless on the mark with the decisive sense and content of their proclamation, which announced Jesus Christ and his kingdom in advance.

Limits of Luther's interpretation of Scripture.

Alongside the Old Testament's promise of Christ and its leading to him, there is also an anticipatory depiction of Christ and his church. Luther finds this above all in the Levitical law, the priesthood, and the sacrificial system, but also in the monarchy. Luther follows here the typology of the Letter to the Hebrews. The Old Testament "pointed to Christ, while the New Testament now gives us what was promised and prefigured in the Old Testament." Christ, then, is present in the figures of the Old Testament.[15] Hence the Old Testament law has a double function, as a model that, on the one hand, points far beyond Christ, and on the other hand, is abolished through Christ and is no longer binding for Christians. Luther applies here a "spiritual interpretation" to the Old Testament that differs from the allegorical, only in that it is grounded in salvation history and explains the relevant texts as pointing to Christ.[16]

Such an interpretation goes beyond the literal meaning of the text. Because Luther does not view these texts as on the same level as the Christian faith, he believes they must be understood in a completely different sense that finds its basis elsewhere. In contrast to the allegorical interpretation, Luther appreciates the literal meaning in his spiritual interpretation because the history these texts deal with is prophetic. Luther is able to place the original literal meaning and the spiritual interpretation together and bring them into living relationship with one another through the concept of symbol, or model. Luther initially sought to interpret a Scripture passage historically in relation to its own contemporary situation and then to relate it to the New Testament community. So, for example, he saw the Passover Feast of the Old Testament as a symbol and model of our Easter feast.[17] In this way, Luther seeks to make the eternal presence of Christ and his salvation meaningful for believers, along with the temporalness of salvation history, which includes the coming of Christ in time. In so doing, he intends to show the essential simultaneity of all believers both before and after Christ, as well as their historical and temporal differentiation.

This interpretation of the Old Testament, however, can no longer be maintained today, just as we can no longer repeat the interpretation of the early Christians. The discovery and introduction of historical exegesis stands between us and these periods. Today, one cannot simply interpret the prophetic texts of the Old Testament christologically, for our understanding of their concrete historical meaning has been sharpened. Their intended meaning was not simply fulfilled in Jesus Christ. Therefore, the relationship of the Old Testament to Christ and to the New Testament has become for us more complicated. Nevertheless, we can agree with Luther that the history of Israel moves toward Christ. If today we as Christians want the Old Testament to be meaningful for us, then we must interpret it christologically, that is, as pointing to Christ. This means that, in contrast to Luther, we must emphasize the historical difference between the two testaments; but in agreement with Luther, we must also emphasize their continuity, that they build on one another.

8

LAW AND GOSPEL

Initially, the distinction between law and gospel sounds typically Lutheran. In the reformed and pietistic streams of Protestantism, which seem to stress the obligating power of the gospel, one often hears the binding demands of the biblical message so much that the gospel is overshadowed and even obliterated. One could say here that the law is merely the flip side of the gospel, which is used to guide the Christian toward a Christlike life. Luther, however, learned firsthand about the disadvantages of the ethos of obligation and compensation of the late Middle Ages, first through his upbringing in popular piety and then through his own experience of monasticism. For this reason, he stressed that God has freed us from all obligations of the law through the gospel. In order not to exchange this newly won freedom for a new legalism, and to emphasize the priority of God's activity, Luther sharply distinguished between law and gospel, but without separating one from the other. He stressed that the Word of God encounters human beings in the twofold form of law and gospel.

ANTITHESIS AND UNITY OF LAW AND GOSPEL

The law has always been known to humans, since God has inscribed it in their hearts at creation. Luther holds this position, as we have seen, in agreement with Paul. Even if the written law had never been given through Moses, the human spirit would have known through its very nature that one should worship God and love one's neighbor. The Spirit of God, according to Luther, dictates the law perpetually into the hearts of all people. But the will of God, which expresses itself in the law and enlivens and enlightens human understanding, has through the sinful desires of human beings been misunderstood ever since the Fall. God was forced, therefore, to give the Israelites a written law through Moses that would remind them of the natural law in their hearts. Moses is not the proper author of the Decalogue but simply the one who interpreted the natural law more clearly.

One must speak of the law in two different ways. The law is the embodiment of the eternal will of God and, as such, is what condemns the sinner. One needs, moreover, to distinguish between the *content* of God's law and the *form* in which this content encounters the sinner. According to its content, the law represents the eternal will of God, and its fulfillment leads human beings to salvation. This means nothing other than that humans shall not impugn or offend God's divinity. If humans conduct themselves accordingly, God will be gracious to them. The law meets humans in their original condition, and it will continue to be valid in the new world to come, where it will be completely fulfilled. Consequently it has protological (original) *and* eschatological (final) significance. The law is always and eternally the unchanging will of God. With the Fall, however, the relationship fundamentally changed between humanity and the law as the eternal will of God. The content remains identical, but the form has changed. This form of the will of God, that is, the law, must now be more thoroughly examined.

The concept of "law" carries with it today a twofold meaning. It has a secular use and a theological or spiritual use. First, it guards against serious transgressions and crimes and protects the public peace in this world, which stands under the influence of the devil and is prone to sin. The law is applied through the offices established by God—namely worldly authorities, parents, and teachers—and also through secular, societal laws. As it manifests itself in this form, humans can essentially fulfill the requirements of God's law and achieve a secular righteousness. It is possible for one to live within the framework of commonly accepted laws without becoming a lawbreaker. One must, however, distinguish this from a second sense or use of the law, which Luther characterizes as the true use. Jesus illustrates this use of the law in his Sermon on the Mount. Through his exposition of the law, he greatly intensified the will of God. A pure heart and perfect obedience are required of people before God. The law, which humans were once able to fulfill, has become for sinners utterly unfulfillable. Instead, the law reveals to them and even intensifies their sinfulness. Hatred of God and despair result from the sinner's knowledge that the requirements of the law cannot be fulfilled. This understanding of the law continually accuses us and delivers us over to wrath, judgment, and eternal death.[1]

All people are to some extent aware of this accusing law of God, but they do not have a genuine knowledge of its power, because they have not yet experienced it. In order for this to be possible, the law must first be preached. Humans will then be startled out of their state of ignorance when they perceive the power of the law, which calls them to repentance. The law, intended as a sign of God's love meant to guide us in a God pleasing life, has become an instrument of God's wrath. This theological aspect of the law shows human beings the extent of their estrangement from God.

Those who wish to preach only the gospel and not the law, because they are afraid it frightens people, refuse to hear God's truth about themselves.

For this reason, Luther opposes the Antinomians, who dispute the theological use of the law and want it to be applied only in the city hall, that is, in the civil domain.[2] For Luther, the law is necessary for salvation, since without the law humans remain far off from God, because they have not recognized just how alienated they already are from God. Through the confrontation with God's wrath and the recognition of their own failure, humans are driven to God and the gospel, for alongside the law stands the gospel, which is the other side of God's Word.

Law and gospel have entirely different, even opposing functions. The law establishes what one should do and what one is not allowed to do, and as a consequence of human failure, it accuses and condemns. The gospel, on the other hand, has as its content God's promise in Christ. It announces that everything the law requires has already been accomplished for us by Christ. The gospel preaches, therefore, the forgiveness of sins: "The preaching of the forgiveness of sins through the name of Christ, that is the gospel."[3] With Paul, from whom Luther has taken over the characterization of the gospel as promise, Luther contrasts law and gospel with one another. The gospel as good news announces the grace of God, that for the sake of Christ, God no longer counts our past failures against us. As Christians we can begin a new life. The law leads to death, but the gospel gives eternal life through the liberation provided by Christ. The law places us under the wrath of God; the gospel, however, brings grace. Law and gospel stand against one another in that through the gospel the justification of the sinner occurs, contrary to what is possible through the law. It is the liberating gospel, not the law, that demands our condemnation and that must be believed. Justification takes place, as Paul says, *apart* from the law. Luther goes still a step further than Paul at this point and says *against* the law.[4]

Law and gospel, however, are related to one another even in their opposition. Law and gospel must indeed be clearly distinguished from one another, but they cannot be separated, just as they also cannot be blended together. They are inseparably connected and bound together. The gospel, which brings with it the forgiveness of sins, presupposes the law and its exposition. Sin is thereby presupposed, but it can only be recognized when one knows the law. Therefore Luther, in his dispute with the Antinomians, could say, "If the law is dismissed, so is sin. If sin is dismissed, so is Christ, for there would be no more need of him."[5] The good news of Christ's saving work and the redemption from sin can neither be understood nor desired if one has not recognized the extent of human estrangement from God, as seen from the vantage point of the law. The gospel needs the law, for it is the preaching of the law that is the indispensable and necessary presupposition of the preaching of the gospel. Without the law, humans cannot realistically judge their own abilities but instead remain self-confident and even arrogant in the assessment of their moral capacity.

As a gracious God, God affects with the law what is alien to him (his alien work) in order to arrive at what is proper to him (his proper work).

The preaching of the law alone, however, does not lead us to true repentance or to belief in the gospel. God's Spirit must work together with the preached word, so we are able to experience the gospel. When the law convinces humans of their sin and they perceive the wrath of God, it drives them to despair. If people hear only the law, they remain in their despair and do not experience salvation. It is therefore important that the word of the gospel be added to the law, so they realize the law is not God's last word but rather points to God's forgiveness and salvation. The law precedes the gospel, that humans find the gospel and flee to Christ. There are not, however, two gods, as believed by Marcion in the second century, one responsible for law and the other offering us the good news of the gospel. Both law and gospel are the work of the same God.

LAW AND GOSPEL AS EXPRESSIONS
OF THE SAME WORD

The law is not exclusively found in the Old Testament, nor is the gospel exclusively found in the New Testament. The law includes everything that reveals our sin to us, accusing our conscience and terrifying us, regardless whether we encounter it in Christ or in Moses. For Luther, the law is not only the explicit imperatives (meaning the accusing and condemning Word of God); he also characterizes the Lord's Prayer as "full of the teaching of the law," since whoever prays it earnestly confesses that he or she has sinned against the law and stands in need of repentance.[6] When we pray "hallowed be your name," for example, we also admit that we have not yet fulfilled this challenge. Thus the Lord's Prayer exercises on us the work of the law.

The preaching of the gospel is, likewise, at the same time the preaching of the law. The preaching of Christ, who should be our example, can take on the character of the preaching of the law, since it manifests the will of God which we are to fulfill. Even the proclamation of Christ as redeemer can become the preaching of the law, since redemption presupposes sin. Yet the gospel also testifies to the goodness of God. People recognize their ingratitude and contempt for the goodness of God, for which they remain indebted. The recognition of sin comes either from the law in the strict sense, that is, from the biblical admonitions and prescriptions, or from the gospel, insofar as it becomes law. Whatever points toward my obligation and shows me I remain guilty, that is the law. The Word of God cannot, consequently, be divided into the words containing law and the words containing gospel, for it is one and the same word that the sinner encounters as law and as gospel. The center of the gospel, being the word of the cross, exposes human sin and lostness more deeply and painfully, for instance, than any law could do. Nevertheless, one can give no other advice to those who have recognized their sin in the face of God's love than to point them to the crucified Christ who bears the sin of the world and brings good news to the poor. This same Christ, to whom we find ourselves ever indebted, is then preached as savior, as the mediator between God and humanity and the comforter of the distressed. The gospel leads to repentance, as well as to faith; it leads to despair and to peace. It is true that law and gospel have two distinct and contrary functions, but both are functions of the same Word of God and occur simultaneously.

Faith is a movement from law toward gospel, a movement that cannot be reversed. As gospel, however, it is a word of comfort, and therefore the movement comes here to rest. The law is taken up into the gospel, but never vice versa. The God and Lord, to whose mercy we are indebted, never ceases to be merciful. The contrast between law and gospel in the life of the sinner indicates, therefore, a transitional stage on the way to the original unity of the two. It also points to the paradoxical situation that the Christian, who has not fulfilled the law and thus stands accused, believes nevertheless in the gospel and fulfills the commandment of God, despite his or her sinfulness. Until now, we have spoken only of sinners. But since the Christian is at the same time sinner and saint, the question arises whether the law has a continuing function for the Christian.

CHRIST AS THE END OF THE LAW

We have seen that Christ is the end of the law. Through him, the will of God, which we are unable to fulfill on our own, is fulfilled vicariously for us. Christ has liberated us from the power of the law, so we are no longer delivered over to the wrath of God and to death. The law as the demand of God, which requires eternal separation from God and thereby death because of our sins, is now fulfilled. The law no longer applies for those who are justified, inasmuch as it accuses and condemns for past offenses. But God's holy will remains in force for them. Yet Christians do not experience this as a requirement of the law, for they freely do what the law requires. Through God's Spirit, who abides in Christians, they willingly fulfill the law. They no longer stand under the demands of the law, but live their lives in accord with God's law through an act of love brought about by the Holy Spirit. The law has recovered its original function. It no longer condemns but yet continues to express God's will.

Although the law meets believers as neither demand nor accusation, and to a certain extent no longer applies to them, it nevertheless has significance for them. First, Christians continue to live their lives on this earth. At the same time, both believers and sinners sometimes live according to the Spirit and sometimes, as Paul says, according to the flesh. To the extent that Christians still belong to their former humanity according to the flesh, the law cannot be invalidated for them but rather reigns accusingly over them. Christians live without the law but also under it. The law, for them, is partly invalidated and in part still valid.

For Christians the decisive event has already taken place, for they have been justified. Yet to the extent they remain their former selves, the law continues to exercise its spiritual or theological function over them and convicts them of their sins. It summons them to overcome their former humanity. Luther makes this clear in his explanation of baptism:

> It signifies that the old Adam in us, together with all sins and evil lusts, should be drowned by daily sorrow and repentance and be put to death, and that the new man should come forth daily and rise up, cleansed and righteous, to live forever in God's presence.[7]

The law serves to overcome the entrenched state of humans and prods them continually to struggle against what leads them astray from God. On earth the struggle for cleansing from sin is never completely successful. We are on the way to fulfilling the law, but this goal will never be accomplished completely. Only at the final resurrection will the law have fulfilled its task and be completely abolished. Concerning the theological function of the law for Christians, however, one must remember they are already moved by the Spirit of God, and repentance is no longer an adverse and difficult matter for them but rather, as Luther said, "something easy and enjoyable."[8] Yet how does one know what one should do? Do not Christians also need the information transmitted through the law so they can know the will of God? To this Luther says two things:

1. If the Holy Spirit moves Christians, they no longer depend on the law. By the power of the Holy Spirit, Christians can establish a new Decalogue, as did Jesus and the apostles.[9] They need no spelled-out precepts, since the Spirit teaches them what to do.

2. Yet Luther qualifies this assertion, admitting that not all Christians possess enough of the Spirit that they can be their own lawmakers. In such individuals, the flesh continues to struggle against the spirit and impedes a clear judgment about the content of God's will. For this reason, it is good for Christians that they orient themselves on the apostolic imperatives of the New Testament. For the Christian, however, these are no longer law but rather apostolic commandments or mandates, that is, directives.[10]

There is, therefore, no theological aspect of the law for Christians, who as those who have been justified, fight no longer against sin but struggle rather to live positive, Christlike lives. For this the New Testament instructions are important, for they lead the Christian to a proper knowledge of good works. To this end, the Decalogue is also useful for the Christian, not in its word-by-word formulation but in the continuing relevance of its content.

As we see in his catechism, Luther expounded the Ten Commandments, freely supplementing and applying it in agreement with biblical admonitions. The Commandments are not only a mirror in which we recognize sin, although they retain this function for the Christian; they are a much needed and wholesome instruction in what God expects from us by way of good works. In contrast to the opinion of later Lutheran orthodoxy and the Reformed tradition, there is, according to Luther, no so-called third use of the law applicable to the one who has been justified. The commandment of God, not the law, provides the Christian with guidance for the right way to live.

9

CHURCH AND SACRAMENT

The Reformation of Martin Luther took place in the context of the struggle with the church of his day. Luther not only opposed the reality of a largely corrupt and superstitious church—he also the Roman, hierarchical, and centralized view of the church. He did not lead the fight on the basis of a churchless, individualistic view of piety, but on the basis of a clear understanding of the gospel on which his view of the church was based. Although the institutional element seems at first to be missing in Luther's descriptions of the church, it has a solid and important place.

The congregation is called together through the Holy Spirit. The church is built by the gospel and is nothing other than the congregation, which is itself gathered around the gospel. The Word of God and the sacraments are distinctive marks of the church: "Where you see baptism, the [eucharistic] bread, and the gospel present, in whatever place and through whatever persons, you must not doubt that there is the church."[1] Luther even goes so far as to state that there can be no salvation outside the church when he says, "I believe no one can be saved who is not found in this congregation, abiding with it harmoniously in one faith, word, sacrament, hope, and love."[2] Faith and community belong inalienably together. One and the same church is visible and invisible, hidden and revealed. It is an institution, as well as the communion of saints. No one can see faith. Therefore, it is only Christ as the good shepherd who knows his sheep. On the other hand, the congregation of believers becomes visible as it gathers around Word and sacrament, as it follows Christ, and as it is led by its pastors.

CHURCH AS COMMUNITY OF SAINTS

Luther inherited the already existing conviction that the church is the communion of saints. For the church of his time, the connection and relationship between the earthly and the heavenly church was important, as seen for example in the veneration of saints and the use of their merits. In contrast to this, the community of saints within the earthly church receded sharply into the background because the biblical word *saint*, in its general catholic sense, was understood as a communion with saints in a meritorious, moralistic manner. Luther brought the communion of saints down from heaven to earth, when in agreement with the New Testament he did not understand "saints" as a particular elite group within the community, but rather as all members of the community, because they are all made holy by God and are all chosen to serve God. Luther no longer distinguished saints from everyday Christians, but rather only deceased saints from living saints. Although he unambiguously concluded that "no saint has adequately fulfilled God's commandments in this life," Luther attributes a living and present significance to the saints for the church, because a living power of faith goes forth from them. They function, therefore, as examples for others to follow.[3]

There is, however, no treasure from the life of the "traditional" saints, no excess of merits they could apply to other Christians, for they lived, suffered, and worked as members of a body together with all other Christians. All petitions directed to the saints in the piety of the time did not, according to Luther, signify that they could achieve something *with* God. They signify instead a gracious work of God *for us* in which God draws us to himself through the service of our fellow saints. To be sure, Luther believed the angels in heaven pray for us as does Christ, but the saints on earth, and perhaps also those in heaven, do that as well. But he will not for this reason call upon the angels and saints in the worship service. In the same way, we do not venerate those on earth who pray for us. Because the justification of believers takes place through God's free and gracious turning to us, our acceptance by God is worked by God alone and needs no intermediary.

The church as communion of saints is at one and the same time gift and responsibility. With Luther, one can summarize the gift of the communion of saints as follows: What belongs to Christ and all the saints belongs also to me, and my burden, distress, and sin is that of Christ and the saints. The faith and prayers of others become a helping force in the powerlessness of my Christian life. I am alone neither in life nor death, for Christ and the church are at my side. Living for oneself ceases in the Christian life and becomes living for one another through love in the community of life. The helping, warning, disciplining, and guiding word of spiritual care we receive in conversation with one another and in the comfort we have from others is important. Luther was thinking here not only of conscious intervention on behalf of one another, but also of possible models for our own life.

The community is also a responsibility, for each person shall take the burden of Christ and his church on themselves. Christians fight for the truth and against injustice, they work for the renewing of the church and its members. They intercede on behalf of the poor with their possessions and on behalf of the sick with their own lives, as well as on behalf of sinners with their own righteousness before God and humankind. Just as Christ took on human form out of love, so we should convert others through the same loving devotion: "Everything we have must be available for service; if it is not available for service, then it is a theft."[4] Every gift and power, as well as possessions, health, and peace, belong to love and to the service of the community. This also holds true in regard to the sinner, from whom we cannot separate ourselves, but whom we must rather seek to lead to Christ. We do not run away but must come running to the center of the church to work for its renewal. That is how Luther understood the path one should take, and it was also the path he sought to follow in his relationship to the church of Rome. Luther saw the community as obligatory, for the unity of the church is to be maintained despite its sin and degeneration.

The term "communion of saints" means evangelical priesthood, that is, service that begins from the gospel. Luther is able to describe his understanding of the church as communion of saints in such a way that he can characterize the priesthood as a law of life for the church. When Christ bears our burdens and intercedes for us with his righteousness, that is a priestly sign from which the mutual upholding and acting on behalf of one another in Christianity is derived. The foundation of the church is the priestly office of Christ, and its inner constitution is the mutual and common priesthood of Christians. Through baptism, all Christians receive their portion of the priestly office. Priesthood means to come before God, to pray for others, to intercede and offer oneself to God, and to proclaim the Word of God to one another. One is never a priest for oneself but always for others. The point of departure for the priesthood of believers, therefore, is the community of saints and not some religious individualism. Public teaching within Christianity is restricted to those called through the congregation. (Individuals may come forward without such a calling, on the other hand, only in mission situations or in an emergency.)

In the private realm, however, each one is called to proclaim the Word of God to others. Luther recognized no congregation that did not proclaim the gospel, and that did not call everyone to give Christian witness or to give spiritual care with a word of comfort to one's neighbor in their time of need. The entire congregation and each of its members has also been fully empowered to declare the forgiveness of sins. This is experienced in private confession and absolution: "When my neighbor comes and says, 'Friend, my conscience is heavy laden, speak the word of absolution to me,' I may of course do that."[5] Luther rejected, to be sure, the churchly obligation of private confession, yet he nonetheless saw in private confession the indispensable form of the gospel. Hearing private confession is a priestly service that can be performed by any Christian. Even when we turn to a called servant of the Word in this regard, we are asking for a brotherly or sisterly service.

OFFICE AND AUTHORITY

There is a twofold foundation of the pastoral office. Although all the baptized are authorized and called to the service of Word and sacrament on the basis of their priesthood, not every member of the congregation can publicly perform these duties for the entire congregation. Such individual self-appointments would lead to chaos in the congregation. In order to guard against this, the congregation must assign these public tasks to a particular person who performs them in the name of the church. In this regard, Luther argued that, according to the New Testament example, Christ has given various people different gifts. Christ has therefore chosen some to be apostles, some to be prophets, some evangelists, and others teachers. The preaching office, therefore, is a position commanded, founded, and ordered by God.

Both these foundations are placed by Luther impartially alongside one another, without connecting them to one another. Although he does not see them as opposites, we must nevertheless be firm in our belief that the pastoral office is founded on, and is a consequence of, the priesthood of all believers. On the other hand, the pastoral office is founded directly by Christ without reference to the priesthood of believers. Both foundations, however, presuppose that the gospel must be proclaimed and the sacraments administered so the church remains as long as the world continues. When one asks who should hold that office, Luther responds with rational and sociological considerations.

The twofold foundation points to a dilemma Luther was most likely aware of, namely that he could not trace the pastoral office back solely to the fact that it was established by Christ. If he were to do that, it would remain inexplicable why it is through baptism that all Christians are made priests. The establishment of the office through Christ would indeed be sufficient in itself. Luther, however, in all of his arguments, is a very practically minded theologian. He recognizes that the preaching office is established by Christ. But from the perspective of proper order, the congregation must now call individual Christians to this special office, to the service of Word and sacrament. In this way the authority the entire congregation and that each individual in it possesses is delegated to a single person chosen out of its midst and called to perform the duties of the office. No one can of his or her own accord claim the authority to carry out this ministry in the congregation. Someone must be called to do so with the consent of the congregation. If these conditions are met, then that person carries out the duties of the office on behalf of the whole congregation.

The pastor is the representative of the congregation who acts in the name of all its members in the proclamation of the gospel and in the liturgy. Luther revealed how he conceptualized this in his description of the evangelical Mass: The pastor chants the words of institution, but the congregation kneels alongside of and around the pastor, for they are all as true and holy priests as the pastor, "for we hear the words of institution publicly and say them along with him in our hearts."[6] The representative action of the pastor, therefore, does not exclude but rather includes the cooperation of the congregation. It is similar with the proclamation of the Word. The public preaching of the pastor to the members of the congregation does not excuse these from their priestly duty to speak the Word of God to one another.

Nonhierarchical understanding of the pastoral office.

The pastoral office has no other content and no other authority than that of the priesthood of all believers, which is founded through baptism. Those who bear the ecclesiastical office act in the name of Christ, their word is the word of Christ, and they represent Christ to the members of their congregation. Yet this is also true of every Christian who exercises spiritual care to another Christian in private confession or ministers to them in some other way. Individual Christians are entrusted with the care of their neighbors; the bearers of the pastoral office, on the other hand, are entrusted with the care of the entire congregation, because their office is of a public character. When Luther speaks of the service of the Word, he characterizes it as the highest office in the church. But he does not think of it in hierarchical terms because he sees it as the task of all Christians.

Luther rejects a special priesthood consecrated through a liturgical rite and emphasizes instead the priesthood of all the baptized. In this way he also deviated from the Jewish practice of retaining special priests. In the New Testament, Luther could not find that the apostles or any other followers of Jesus were designated as priests. This title was instead applied without distinction to all Christians. This strict functional understanding of the pastoral office also highlights what was once considered its inalienable character; there is no special priestly class.

Proper calling.

Decisive for the pastoral call is the proper liturgical action with which one is called to be a preacher of the gospel. One cannot take the office by oneself, but receives it through proper and public appointment. Luther emphasizes the proper calling, as it is expressed in the *Augsburg Confession* (1530), especially over the enthusiasts who believed themselves to be appointed directly from God.[7] He also sought thereby to defend against Roman Catholic accusations that his Reformation would bring about chaotic conditions.

Yet Luther distinguished between two types of calling: an internal, immediate call (as when God called the prophets and the apostle Paul directly) and an external, mediated call (which comes from God through human beings). An immediate call must be demonstrated through external signs and evidences. Luther applied this against Thomas Müntzer and the enthusiast peasants. When God breaks through the pattern of the historical order, this must be confirmed through external signs and wonders. The external call mediated through other people, on the other hand, does not need these signs, for it takes place when someone is sought out by other Christians to preach and is given the pastoral office. Of course, it is ultimately God who calls someone to be a pastor through other Christians.

The proper calling of a pastor is not only necessitated for the sake of churchly order, but also for the sake of the pastor. In this way pastors are able to know that their office is not self-appointed but has been entrusted to them. Luther speaks here from personal experience. In his work as a reformer, he was comforted by the knowledge that he did seek out the pastoral office but was called to it: "For I would surely in the long run lose courage and fall into despair if . . . I had undertaken these great and serious matters without call or commission."[8] If one appoints oneself to be a preacher, then that is disobedience against God: "It is the calling and commission that make the parish pastor and preacher. . . . God doesn't want anything done by one's own choice or notion, but by command and calling, especially in regard to the pastoral office."[9] Luther is aware that many people rebel against this rule because they believe themselves to be especially well suited to the pastoral office. Yet Luther challenges such people to consider that if God needs them, then God will call them.

How the call takes place for each person is not important. What is important is that the call comes according to human order and not a divine order. It is also important for Luther that congregations have the power to chose their servants of the Word. At the same time, the bishops, according to the example of the New Testament, should also play a role in this process when they take their office seriously. Yet they dare not appoint someone without the consent of the congregation: "Calling is done legitimately by the church," whereby the church always assumes the cooperation of the local congregation.[10] Luther, therefore, shows that he is no longer interested in a special liturgical act of ordination. Ordination, in principle, is nothing other than the calling and commission to the pastoral office.

Church and tradition.

For Luther it was clear that the Protestants were not building a separate church, but instead "are the true old church, and with the entire holy Christian church are one body and one communion of saints," for God has wonderfully preserved the true church even in the midst of its Babylonian captivity.[11] Even through the fall of the papacy, Luther did not believe the established church would be lost. He found in the Roman Mass, for instance, alongside what was contrary to the gospel, what was genuinely Christian, and these elements he took up in his German Mass. He also took up many Latin hymns and sung portions of the liturgy and translated them into German. An example of this is the Advent hymn, "Savior of the Nations, Come."[12] He approached the German hymns of the Middle Ages in a similar manner, cleansing them of thoughts contrary to the gospel and sometimes substituting new verses. This can be seen, for example, in the Christmas hymn, "All Praise to You, Eternal Lord."[13]

Luther was especially brought to reflect on the authority of tradition in the church in his disputes with the Anabaptists. He stressed that a consensus of the whole church was binding, so long as the teaching or practice in question did not contradict Scripture. He objected, for instance, to the spiritualistic interpretation of the Lord's Supper by Thomas Müntzer and Huldreich Zwingli, and argued that the testimony of the entire Christian church was already sufficient reason to remain with the Reformation understanding of the Lord's Supper. He found it dangerous and frightful to abolish something that had, as a basic consensus, "existed harmoniously throughout all the world for more than 1,500 years."[14] Luther restricted neither Christian dogma nor the teachings of the church to what is expressly found in the Bible. In contrast to the Reformed camp of Calvin and Zwingli, he did not reduce the truth content of Christianity to biblical teaching alone, because he recognized that the Holy Spirit has also been active in the church since the time of the apostles. On this basis, the validity of Christian tradition is established, yet it must be critically examined to be sure it does not contradict the clear truth of the gospel found in Scripture. Whatever stands up under this examination should be retained. In this sense, Scripture is the standard against which the tradition of the church is measured, and not vice versa.

If, however, in particular cases tradition is not able to be harmonized with Scripture or stands in obvious contradiction to it, then it must be rejected. Such a "no" to tradition was especially painful for Luther because, by rejecting tradition, he brought the entire development of the church into question and was confronted with the dangerous possibility that he was opposing the church of Christ and even Christ himself. Luther confesses that "no one likes to say the church is in error; and yet, if the church teaches anything in addition or contrary to the Word of God, one must say that it is in error."[15] The question remains, nevertheless, What precisely does Luther understand by "Word of God" in this context? Even Scripture passages thought to ground or introduce teachings Luther rejected were held up to him as the "Word of God."

Authority of the Word of God.

Neither the Bible, nor the canon as such, nor individual Scripture passages are able to serve for Luther as the final authority and binding standard. Instead, only the center of Scripture, the gospel as understood through Christ, can serve this function. As we have already seen, Luther viewed the canon, as a piece of the tradition of the church that must be subject to the scrutiny of the Word of God. This canonical criticism is to be distinguished from subjective and arbitrary decisions that pick out individual words or verses and hold them to be absolute. Luther, in contrast, argues on the basis of the core of the Bible, namely the theocentric character of the gospel. From this perspective the glory of God, who creates without preconditions out of nothing, is to be defended.

Alongside and apart from the Word of God, there is no authority in the church, for Luther, that has unconditional validity. When someone calls on the opinion of the church, the decisive point is whether this opinion is based on the middle of Scripture or is only being passed off as the true opinion of the church. The first has authority, the latter has none. The teachings of the church, the opinions of the church fathers, and the traditions and offices of the church cannot have unconditional authority because the church can err. According to Luther, this is demonstrated by the Bible itself, for David and Nathan in the Old Testament erred, and the apostles often sinned or failed. In Luther's view, the church remains "a submissive sinner before God until the day of judgment and is holy alone in Christ its Savior by grace and the forgiveness of sins."[16] A Christian cannot offer unconditional obedience to the church but rather only to the gospel proclaimed by the church. Luther observes that already in New Testament times, Paul reproaches Peter because of his deviations from the gospel (Galatians 2). Authority and the duty of obedience toward the church have both their foundation and their limits in the gospel: "To err is human" goes also for the church, for in this point it has no privileged position in comparison to earthly authorities. Even in regard to the proclamations of councils, it must be determined and not taken for granted that they attest the truth, even though the entire church speaks through them. They attest the truth only when they are grounded on the gospel.

For Luther, the true church of Christ and historical Christianity are not the same thing. The true church is hidden and is not identical to the official church and its history. Often it is not even recognized by the official church. The true and hidden church is nevertheless ruled by the spirit of Christ. It cannot err, because Christ remains by it, and it remains with Christ until the end of the world. Yet the historical church and the hidden church have the same focal points of identity: the gospel and the sacraments. Even in the often erring official church, the true church continually becomes visible when the former holds firm to the gospel and allows it to work unhindered.

THE SACRAMENTS

Martin Luther largely follows Augustine in his understanding of the sacraments. He describes a sacrament as a visible sign of God's invisible grace. Although every visible action has some meaning and can be understood as a picture or image of an invisible reality, this does not mean that every symbolic action is a sacrament. A symbolic action has sacramental character only when it is instituted by God and is connected with a promise. Where there is no divine word of promise (as in the case of marriage or confirmation), one cannot, in Luther's view, call these sacraments. On the other hand, there are divine promises such as prayer and making the sign of the cross for which there is no corresponding symbol. These, too, are not sacraments. According to Luther's understanding, therefore, only Baptism and the Lord's Supper are sacraments in the strict sense. In them the signs instituted by God and a promise, namely the forgiveness of sins, meet. The special quality of a sacrament is found in its visibility. The visibility of the sacraments is an aid to faith, for in them one can see through their symbolic character the promises of God for individuals. Luther explains how signs and promise work together in *The Small Catechism*. In regard to Baptism he wrote, "It is not the water that produces these effects, but the Word of God connected with the water."[17] Similarly he wrote concerning the Lord's Supper, "Eating and drinking do not in themselves produce them [great effects], but the words 'for you' and 'for the forgiveness of sins.'"[18] The promise that joins with the sign invites one to faith. A sacrament does not function automatically through its occurrence, but it demands and fosters faith.

In contrast to the Roman Catholic teaching of his time on sacraments, Luther stressed that the sacraments were not necessary for salvation. Yet a Christian will never despise them. If one is able to receive baptism, then one should be baptized. If conditions, however, prevent someone from being baptized, then that person will nevertheless be saved if they believe in the gospel. Baptism is "only" a particular form of offering the gospel. The same is true with regard to the Lord's Supper. Opposing the Anabaptists and the spiritualists, it was necessary for Luther to point out that the sacraments are not mere external matters one can reject, but that they are instituted by God, who has commanded that they be made use of appropriately. One dare not tear sacrament and gospel from one another, putting one down as mere external trapping while lifting up the other. Word and sacrament, or gospel and sacrament, are two ways God relates to us.

Baptism.

Baptism by water is first of all a human action. Yet humans do not baptize in their own name but in the name of God. Baptism brings a complete salvation, as Luther says in *The Small Catechism*: "It affects forgiveness of sins, delivers from death and the devil, and grants eternal salvation to all who believe."[19] Baptism is singular and unrepeatable. Yet although it is a one time act, it remains present throughout one's life and must continually be accepted: "The Christian life is nothing other than a daily baptism; once begun, we keep going back for more."[20] The new life given through the external act of baptism must be continually turned into a reality. God makes a covenant with human beings in baptism and agrees to forgive all their sins. The symbolic action in baptism, being immersed or washed with water, is to be sure, a one time occurrence, but it must be continually actualized: "The old Adam in us . . . should be drowned by daily sorrow and repentance and put to death, and the new man should come forth daily and rise up."[21] Luther, building on Romans 6, emphasizes the lifelong realization and fulfillment of baptism. While Paul speaks of a baptism of the converted, Luther has in mind infant baptism, in which the great moment of decision and insight into life are missing, and the emphasis is on the fact that baptism should be realized throughout the whole of one's life. If one falls from baptism, then repentance is not a new, supplemental means of grace, but rather affects a return to one's baptism and to the promise that took place within it.

Discussion of infant baptism.

Infant baptism was especially opposed by the Anabaptists. Luther brought forth all manner of arguments against their rejection of infant baptism. He argued, for instance, that God would not have allowed it to continue so long it was not right.[22] He was also of the opinion that Christianity would not have existed if infant baptism was false and against God's will, because in such a case there would have been no legitimate baptism. But this, however, would contradict the confessional statement: "I believe in one holy Christian church." Luther referred to the force of tradition, which says we should not eliminate or change anything unless there is clear scriptural witness against it. Luther conceded, however, that infant baptism was not expressly instituted or commanded in Scripture. Instead, baptism alone is commanded, an instruction that does not limit itself to adult baptism. Because the Anabaptists are a more recent development, the burden of evidence rests on them, and they need clear scriptural testimony for their rejection of infant baptism. For those who retain infant baptism, it is sufficient that Scripture does not say anything against the baptism of infants and that it is in accordance with Scripture. Also in regard to infant baptism, Luther does not back away from the generally accepted conviction that the sacraments are effective only when they are received in faith. The faith and confession of the baptismal sponsors contribute nothing to the sanctification of the one baptized, because no one is saved through the faith of other people but only through one's own faith.

Luther never based the validity of infant baptism on the presence of faith in the infant, although he did for a time argue that such faith existed. Infants are to be baptized, not because it is clear that they believe but because it is in accordance with Scripture. One also cannot baptize infants on the basis of their future faith. Luther ultimately argues that baptism calls one to faith, and the reality and validity of baptism do not depend on the faith of the one being baptized. Baptism is entirely the work of God in which God, nevertheless, expects the assent of the one baptized. Even in the case of a "believer's baptism," where baptism is made dependent on the faith of the baptismal candidate, it remains unclear when one should baptize. One can never know with certainty whether the one to be baptized truly believes. There is no reliable sign of faith, not even the free decision to present oneself for baptism nor the confession of faith by the candidate. One always builds on a foundation of uncertainty with regard to believers' baptism. To baptize and to have oneself baptized on the basis of one's own faith not only makes for uncertainty but it is also idolatry, for one relies on one's own work rather than the action of God through which God accepts us. So it is, according to Luther, that the baptism of the Anabaptists is reduced to a mere sign of their piety. Yet faith and baptism nevertheless belong together. Faith clings to the promise of God that one may baptize and that through baptism God receives the one baptized into his covenant. Faith, however, is also the consequence of baptism in which one affirms what has taken place in baptism.

The Lord's Supper.

In the development of his doctrine of baptism, Luther in principle only separated himself from the righteousness of the Anabaptists and often that of those who held to the so-called old faith, as well. Yet in the development of his doctrine of the Lord's Supper, one can distinguish between two different lines of his thought. Up until about 1524, Luther's argumentation was directed against Rome, against the teaching of the sacrifice of the Mass. After this time, he battled against the enthusiasts and the Swiss, that is, against the Reformed camp and their symbolic interpretation of the Lord's Supper. The Roman church held to a doctrine of transubstantiation, which teaches that in the Eucharist the inner substance of bread and wine is transformed to body and blood. Luther, in contrast, maintained a doctrine of consubstantiation, which affirms that the body and blood of Christ are present in unchanged bread and wine. Yet he did not place any great weight or significance on this difference.

As late as 1520, he said that whoever wished was free to retain the doctrine of transubstantiation, but that he would not tolerate anyone making this opinion an article of faith that others must accept.[23] Important for Luther was that in the eating and drinking of bread and wine, union with Christ and all the saints took place. The resultant actual presence of the body and blood of Christ (real presence) was important for Luther inasmuch that, as a sign of Christ's sacrificial death, it assures us of the forgiveness of sins.

Words of institution.

The eucharistic words of institution were decisive for Luther. Important in this regard is not only the New Testament text itself but also Luther's understanding of the gospel, which he used to interpret the text—an understanding that itself confirmed the gospel's promise of grace. In our understanding of the Lord's Supper, reason must not be made to rule over the text, because God, who makes himself understood in the text, is greater than our reason. The text must take precedence as God's Word of promise. Faith also means that we must cast our own thoughts and desires behind us and hold on, as if we were blind, to the will of God. Luther writes,

> A faithful, God fearing heart does this: it asks first whether it is God's Word. When it hears that it is, it smothers with hands and feet the question, Why is it useful or necessary? For it says with fear and humility, "My dear God, I am blind; truly I know not what is useful or necessary for me, nor do I wish to know, but I believe and trust that thou dost know best and dost intend the best in thy divine goodness and wisdom. I am satisfied and happy to hear thy simple Word and perceive thy will."[24]

Luther stressed the sovereignty of the Word and will of God over against all human insight into religious necessity and the meaning of divine actions. What God's Word says and gives is useful to us, and we cannot measure God's Word according to what we determine to be its usefulness. We must follow the literal meaning of the text and not some human interpretation, for the wording of the text is in all events given by God.

Real presence of Christ.

Luther fought with unexpected stubbornness for the real presence of Christ in the Lord's Supper. His specific interest in the issue was the same as what he championed against Rome: the sacrament must be understood as a genuine gift of God that comes to us without human assistance, and that means also without the help of faith. What is essential in the real presence is that Christ

encounters us in such a way that here pure passivity and pure reception domi-
nate the action on the human side. Although Christ is likewise personally
present in the oral proclamation of the Word, in Holy Communion he is
physically present for the individual. Analogous to the way the Word becomes
flesh, this bodily presence is at the same time a spiritual presence, for everything
that takes place in faith is spiritual because faith receives Christ's presence.
Spiritual eating means not only to savor something that is spiritual, but also to
partake of a genuine reality that comes from the Holy Spirit and desires to be
received spiritually, that is, in faith. There is, therefore, no pure, inner, spiritual
presence of Christ. Christ's presence manifests itself instead in what is outwardly visible, in bread and wine. Whoever despises this external presence also
denies that God has revealed himself to us outwardly in human history. When
Luther's opponents felt the real presence of Christ in bread and wine on the
altar was unworthy of God, Luther could only understand this as a rejection of
God's becoming flesh in the incarnation.

Through the power of the word of Christ, his body and blood are present
in Holy Communion. The body of Christ is present in the bread and wine, and
is received by all, not only those who believe. But only for the latter does it
work for their salvation, for the others, who reject Christ, it works for their
damnation. The "concretizing" of grace in the bodily presence of Christ thus
brings either life or death. In the Sacrament of the Altar, the believer receives
the forgiveness of sins, because the sacrifice of Christ is present in the sacrament.
In believers, the gospel affects "forgiveness of sins, life, and salvation," as Luther
puts it in *The Small Catechism*.[25] Luther does not speak at all in this regard of the
real presence. It is instead a fundamental presupposition of the efficacy of the
sacrament, for someone can only be efficacious when that person is really present. The real presence, therefore, is not an object of faith but rather a fundamental presupposition of the salvation one receives in Holy Communion.

EXCURSUS: ADDITIONAL ACCENTS IN
LUTHER'S THEOLOGY

When we turn our attention from our survey of Luther's teachings, some might
ask, "But didn't Luther have anything to say about human sinfulness, the person
of Christ and his work of reconciliation, or eternal life?" Of course, Martin
Luther made many comments on these areas in his writings, and in so doing set
out important new accents in their treatment. Yet for the most part, they are
developed out of his foundational Reformation perspective, as we have seen in
the preceding treatment. We highlight here only a few points.

1. In his understanding of the figure of Jesus Christ, Luther largely followed ancient Christian dogma. It is a noteworthy quality of Luther that, as a former Augustinian monk, he not only took up Augustine in many facets but also took up many suggestions from the whole of the ancient church in his understanding of the message of the New Testament. For Luther it was clear that Jesus Christ was truly human and truly divine, and he held fast to the two-natures Christology of the ancient church. Nevertheless, it was essential for him that Jesus, as the human face of God, allows us a direct look into the heart of God. Luther conceded that Muslims knew much about God, such as that God is creator, sustainer, and redeemer. Yet he maintained that we can have certainty that this God is also our redeemer only through Jesus Christ. Luther's interest in the nature of Jesus Christ was not speculative but instead was directly existential. Christ opens for us the entrance to the heart of God and thereby to God himself. In such statements, we see Luther turning toward an understanding of Jesus as redeemer and moving away from the medieval understanding of Christ as judge of the world. Luther did not see in Christ a figure that evoked fear, but rather the Son of God, who offered himself for us and who brings us salvation. This salvation is necessary for human beings, because in our estrangement from God, there are no possibilities for us to be justified before God.

2. Luther emphasizes in his understanding of humanity that human beings, in relation to the created order, possess a large degree of freedom. As creatures of God endowed with reason, humans can move in the world, conscious of their responsibility and can lead happy and successful lives. But because they are estranged from God, their success in the world, whether brought about through human self-elevation or through denial of the world, does not bring them a single step closer to God. In principle, all human works lead to a heightening of human sinfulness. They are an expression of human self-affirmation and do not give glory to God but to human beings. Through them we seek to forget we ultimately owe everything to God. This complete dependence on God is also emphasized in Luther's doctrine of justification.

3. Together with Augustine, Luther affirmed that because of our sinfulness we have earned nothing but eternal death and eternal alienation from God. Yet Christ has died on account of our sins. He placed himself where, by all rights, we should have stood, in a state of estrangement from God and damnation. Through this wonderful exchange in which he took our place, an alien justification has been attributed to us and as undeserving sinners we have been pronounced justified. Jesus Christ bridges the horribly wide chasm between people and God. As the human face of God, he takes our side so we can once more find ourselves on the side of God and inherit peace with God and eternal life. This saving event is so unexpected and unusual that it is not able to be deduced from any empirical facts, but can only be comprehended in faith alone through the gospel, that is, through trust in God's promise. Because this unexpected gift of eternal life is opened up to us, Luther is able to look with different eyes on eternal judgment and the end of the world, a subject that also drew the attention of most of his contemporaries.

4. *The piety of the late Middle Ages was characterized by the fear of the last judgment, because there we are met by the merciless judge of the world before whom we are not able to endure.* Luther, in contrast, was able to speak of the "dear last day," the advent of which he longingly awaited.[26] At the end of the world there is no merciless day of accounting that awaits us, but we encounter as judge the same Jesus Christ whom we have already experienced in faith as our redeemer. To be sure, Luther took repentance seriously and even heightened its importance by stressing that the entire life of a Christian must be one of continual repentance, and that we must ever flee to the grace of God. Yet he did not live under the anxiety of a manufactured illusion that, to the very end of his life, he had to make himself acceptable to God through radical penitential exercises. Luther knew that such efforts were useless and put his trust, instead, in the grace of God offered to us apart from any human merit. A life of repentance should demonstrate that our life on earth is one of continual new beginnings and is always in need of improvement. He also saw himself inspired to this Christlike life because humans live *from* the grace of God that makes daily life possible, and they live *toward* the grace of God that opens for them the fullness of new life. The Christian life should be one of thankfulness marked by many and great good works. The ethical orientation of the Christian life is not the prerequisite but rather the result of faith. This practical consequence will be elucidated in the following chapters, in which we examine two areas of ethical reflection.

10

LOVE, MARRIAGE, AND PARENTHOOD

It is, according to Luther, the good will of God and God's own work that humans exist in this world as male and female. Because of this, one sex should not attempt to belittle or hold the other in contempt but instead honor the other as a good work that is pleasing to God. God has ordered things so that men and women are mutually dependent upon one another. Even the attraction and desire for the other, that is to say, sexual love, is a work of God:

> And that is the Word of God, through the power of which in the human body seed becomes fruit and the intense natural attraction to the woman is created and preserved. This cannot be hindered either with vows or with laws for it is God's Word and work.[1]

This has been true since the beginning of the creation and remains unchanged today. Luther speaks with lofty words of the love between the sexes for it is the greatest and purest among all the various types of earthly love. He contrasts it not only to false love that seeks egoistically after its own self but also to the natural love that exists between parents and children and among siblings: "Every other love seeks something other than that which it loves, but this love alone desires to have only the one loved. And if Adam had not fallen then the loveliest thing imaginable would have been a bride and groom."[2]

But Adam did fall and humanity thereby has fallen into sin. This also affects sexual love, which is no longer pure. It is no longer a pure giving to the other but now also seeks to satisfy its own lusts on the other. Sexual lust has even had its effect upon procreation. Luther understands Psalm 51:5, "Indeed, I was born guilty, a sinner when my mother conceived me," as evidence of the transmission of original sin, which is connected with the human act of procreation and not (as is common in modern exegesis), as a statement concerning the historical fate of Israel.[3] Luther remained trapped, therefore, in the traditional Augustinian contempt for sexual lust. Yet despite the limitations of this viewpoint Luther recognized that there is a demonic element of egoistic desire in sexual love in which the one partner only uses the other instead of, as Luther explained in his explanation of the sixth commandment, to love and honor them.[4] Luther understands marriage, therefore, within the framework of this complex of problems brought about by original sin.

MARRIAGE

Luther determined first of all that marriage was already the will and work of God before the Fall. It was not an emergency measure meant to limit human sinfulness. God established marriage so that the world would be filled with human beings. Although for Luther it was clear that marriage and children belong together, he in no way saw the meaning of marriage restricted to procreation. In our fallen world marriage also means assistance for us sinners and a means of healing in the face of the promiscuity of the sex drive and also help against the disorder that comes over us because of sin. Marriage harnesses the sexuality distorted by sin and defends body, goods, honor, and friendship from the harm that unbridled sexuality brings upon us. According to Luther, marriage can not be lived without sin because sensual desire continues within marriage. Nevertheless, he insists that marriage is the will of God, a holy order that stands under God's blessing.

Marriage, sensuality, and celibacy.

God does not judge those who stand in faith and wish to do God's will in spite of the sensual desires that take place in marriage. Hence despite the sin associated with it, marriage (if not by its nature then by the grace of God) receives God's gracious word of creation, forgiveness, and justification. Also in sin it remains a godly and holy estate. Luther sees sexual love, therefore, from a two-fold perspective: from the perspective of God's good creation, and from the perspective of its distortion through sin.

Marriage, according to Luther, is the fundamental order of God from which all other orders and states are derived. It is commanded through God's creative will, for humans are driven to it by their very nature. Marriage cannot, therefore, simply be understood as God's command, but rather, by design of the creator, it is a necessary part of being human. Whoever does not enter into the estate of matrimony at some point, according to Luther, inevitably falls prey to a loss of sexual discipline, prostitution, or self-abuse. These opinions are colored by Luther's own experiences with and observations of celibacy and contain a great deal of criticism specific to his time. So it is that Luther can also contend that the one who withholds himself from the estate of matrimony tempts God and does the will of Satan. Only within marriage is sexuality not a destructive force. Hence everyone should enter into the estate of marriage, if for no other reason, then out of necessity and because of the sin inherent in our sexuality.

Yet Luther is aware of exceptions to marriage that are conceded by God. In the first place, there are some people who by their very nature are simply not suited to marriage. Likewise, there are others to whom God gives the exalted and gift of abstinence so that they are able to live a chaste life without being married. Such people, however, are very rare. According to Luther, we would not find one among 1,000 people, for such a person is a "special miracle of God."[5] The Roman church leaders lost sight of this fact when they made priestly celibacy into law. Yet if some genuinely have this gift from God, they should be thankful. No one, however, should put their trust in such abstinence and attempt the celibate life unless God has called them specially to be single, or unless they feel God's gracious gift of abstinence very strongly in themselves.

Luther, therefore, conceded the possibility of a celibate state and emphasized its special function and worth. While it was a sin in the Old Testament to be without wife and child, this no longer applies for the New Testament. In agreement with Paul, Luther is even able to admit that the single state is better inasmuch as one, without the responsibilities of marriage,

> may better be able to preach and care for God's Word. . . . It is God's Word and the preaching which make celibacy—such as that of Christ and Paul—better than the estate of marriage. In itself, however, the celibate life is far inferior.[6]

That means, then, that from the moral perspective there is no higher estate than that of matrimony. Luther rejected, therefore, the qualitative supremacy of the priestly estate. The marital estate, according to Luther, through the burdens that God lays on those who are married, provides innumerable opportunities to express patience and love that a single person does not have. Hence marriage is the rule and the celibate life is the exception.

One should enter happily into marriage and should remain happy in marriage because we know that God is pleased with marriage and with those who are married. The marital estate is adorned and made holy with the Word of God. Hence marriage is a powerful source of joy in the midst of all burdens, crises, and disappointments. In marriage one finds peace in suffering, desire in apathy, and happiness in sorrow: "It is an art to see this estate according to the Word of God that alone makes both the estate of matrimony and those who enter into it lovely."[7] Luther therefore rejects the secular view of marriage that sees it only as a human and worldly institution that has nothing to do with God. Marriage is sanctified through God's will and word.

Seen from the perspective of human beings, however, marriage can only be holy when it is lived in the knowledge of God's involvement, that is, in faith. This does not contradict the characterization of marriage as an external, physical, or worldly thing, for even Luther is able to refer to marriage as a "worldly business."[8] Marriage belongs to God's natural created order and not to Christ's redemptive order. Hence marriage is not a sacrament but is instead an institution that stands under God's blessing. Marriage is a holy estate even with those who are not Christians. Because it falls under the natural order, however, the church is not responsible for marriage as a legal institution. Marriage should not be subject to ecclesiastical laws and judgments but rather to those of the secular order. So it is that in those lands that adopted the Lutheran Reformation the legal aspects of marriage are administered by the secular authorities. The church cannot establish laws in regard to this natural order of God any more than did Christ or the apostles, explained Luther. The only exception found in those matters is when the issue at hand is one of conscience. Here there is also a place for the pastor to counsel and if necessary comfort people when they are uncertain about something in their own conscience and are confused or when they have violated the true estate of marriage.

One sees the consequences of the doctrine of the two kingdoms in Luther's understanding of marriage. Marriage is part of the created order and is therefore a worldly thing that belongs to the kingdom of the left. It is not a part of God's redemptive order for one can also be sanctified without marriage. Hence the question of what form marriage should take (patriarchal, partnership based, or egalitarian) must be solved in the secular realm and one to which the church is not able to contribute any special knowledge. The form of marriage is determined by the social conditions of different ages. Hence Martin Luther's wife, Katharina, was alone responsible for the family's home, property, and finances while her husband pursued his theological responsibilities. Both parents were responsible for the upbringing of the children, Katharina mostly during the day and when her husband was away on business, and Luther mostly after he came home from work and when his wife was sick, although the children were allowed to play around his desk while he was working. There was no clear separation of household duties, for during his many years before marriage, Martin Luther had learned, for instance, to mend his own clothing, a practice he happily continued after his marriage despite the protests of his wife. It was clear, however, according to the custom of the time, that he would represent the family in important external matters, as for instance when a salary increase needed to be sought from the elector. Katharina, on the other hand, was mostly responsible for internal matters, which included supervision of those employed within the household.

Although Luther on principle was supposed to have nothing to do with marital problems in his pastoral duties, as this was the responsibility of the secular authorities, he nevertheless gave advice on specific questions when asked in order to give counsel to the conscience. He frequently dealt with marital problems in his letters in a pastoral manner. According to Luther, the real responsibility of the pastoral office in regard to marriage was to proclaim to those who had entered into this estate not only the gospel but also God's will for marriage. It should, therefore, announce to them the power of faith and of love, without which one cannot have a good marriage.

The practice of marriage.

In the practice of marriage, Luther continued the traditional division of the marital union. The actual marriage, that is, the pronouncement of the couple as husband and wife, took place before the door of the church. Inside the church, at the altar, the spiritual ceremony took place in which God's Word concerning marriage was proclaimed, God's blessing announced, and the prayers of the congregation for the young couple sought: "The pastor in this way blesses the bride and groom, confirms their marriage, and testifies that they have accepted and publicly acknowledged each other."[9] The church wedding is therefore only a confirmation of the marriage that has already taken place and is a belated act of ecclesiastical blessing.[10]

The public nature of marriage belongs to its very essence. Luther was careful to ensure that marriage as a public estate was always celebrated with a wedding before witnesses and the local congregation. A secret engagement and marriage, according to Luther, provides no certainty and the testimony of both the parties is not sufficient to recognize their marriage. A marriage should also not take place without the knowledge and consent of the parents, for this would violate the Fourth Commandment. On the other hand, parents should not force their children into a marriage against their will, nor should they forbid them to marry when they fall in love with someone.

Marriage has a twofold meaning in the relationship of the couple to each other and in their responsibility to procreate and rear children. Husband and wife are first of all there for one another. The happiness of a marriage is secured when "husband and wife cherish one another, become one, [and] serve one another."[11] Sensual love alone is not enough for it can quickly cool. Marriage is much more a covenant of faithfulness:

> That is the ground and the entire essence of marriage, that a person gives him or herself to another and promises to remain faithful to them and not to turn to another. Meanwhile the one, therefore, is bound to the other and gives him or herself over captive to the other.[12]

Within this covenant of faithfulness, sexuality has a different context than outside of marriage, for it is no longer driven by self-seeking lust but by the desire to serve the other. The physical relationship of a couple need not be limited only to that which is necessary to produce children. God allows couples sexual intercourse beyond what is necessary for procreation as an expression and consummation of marital love. Here Luther provides a corrective to Paul by contending:

> Although Christian married folk should not permit themselves to be governed by their bodies in the passion of lust, as Paul writes to the Thessalonians [I Thessalonians. 4:5], nevertheless each one must examine himself so that by his abstention he does not expose himself to the danger of fornication and other sins.[13]

Marital love and faithfulness guard against disappointment in one's spouse, in times of conflict, and in the event that one's spouse is unbearable and mean-spirited. Luther viewed marriage very soberly and recognized that it is always endangered when it is lived only by its own power. A Christian, however, does not draw superficially upon happiness, but upon the will of God. Luther argues similarly when he speaks of the illness of a spouse that prevents the fulfilling of conjugal duty. In this situation, one should not separate from the spouse but should serve God in the person of the one who is sick: "Blessed and twice blessed are you when you recognize such a gift of grace and therefore serve your invalid . . . [spouse] for God's sake."[14] We can trust God, that we will not be given more than we are able to bear. Everything depends on whether one enters and continues in marriage with God, or self-confidently, that is, without God.

A first love or an initial falling in love is not, according to Luther, a sufficient foundation for a marriage: "It's easy enough to get a wife, but to love her with constancy is difficult."[15] It is an act of the devil that one becomes weary of one's spouse and casts his or her eye upon others. One should arm oneself against this danger by beginning and leading a marriage under the eyes of God and praying for God's help. If another woman seems to me more beautiful and desirable than my own wife, wrote Luther, then I say to myself, "I have at home a much more beautiful ornament in the person of my own wife who God has given me and made beautiful above all others, even if she were physically unattractive or otherwise frail."[16]

The other aspect of marriage, according to the Word and will of God, is its fruitfulness. Here the mother serves the loving will of God for his creature. She is made worthy with her whole being to be the tool and hand of God. This is true in pregnancy as well as with birth, seen in light of the crisis and danger of death associated with child-bearing that Luther poignantly experienced as a result of the state of medicine and hygiene in his time. What the natural person sees as pure burden, limitation, and hard work, the eye of faith sees as a unique calling to serve God's gracious will and to foster new life. God therefore calls on parents to be apostles, bishops, and pastors of their children.

PARENTHOOD AND FAMILY

Parents, according to Luther, represent God and deserve to be seen by their children as the highest authority on earth. All other human authority, including that of the secular rulers, is derived from parental authority. Parental authority extends across both regiments. The parents are the rulers of their children in the secular regiment. By virtue of the priesthood of all believers, however, they are also the spiritual authority for their children and are responsible to proclaim the gospel to them. Hence parents should not only love their children and prepare them for success in secular society, but they should also provide for them spiritually as they are able. Through a good upbringing, parents can earn blessedness for their children—or through neglect, damnation.

Luther did not think highly of the opinion, that has now become popular, that one should not seek to influence children, that is, that they should decide for themselves what they wish to believe. Although he constantly stressed that one cannot and dare not force someone to believe, he was well aware of the role parents have as models and of the truth of the proverb: "The apple does not fall far from the tree." If the parents do not have a positive relationship of faith then the children, whether consciously or not, will be brought up with an attitude of religious indifference. God, however, has established parents as his representatives. For this reason children should see their parents as representing God. Hence Luther wrote in his *Small Catechism* that children should hold their parents in honor, for to honor is greater than to love.[17] To honor, however, also belongs love, and beyond this respect. Love should not occur apart from respect and respect not apart from love for both should be given to one's parents just as to God. To do justice to the parent-child relationship we must first of all remember that parents are the highest unified authority their children know. This authority, however, is not grounded in any parental claim to power for this authority finds its limits in the divine commission of the parents.

Luther attributes broad powers to the father as head of the household. In addition to the parents and children, a family of the late Middle Ages frequently included servants, journeymen, apprentices of the craftsmen, or boarders, all under one roof. In the relationship between husband and wife, the husband is the head, as Luther deduces from the physical and spiritual situation of both parties. Yet none of the normal tasks of wives are below the dignity of a husband to perform when necessary. Hence Luther can describe how the husband at night rocks the children, washes diapers, and cares for and works for his wife.[18]

The wife is the companion of the husband. She carries out the normal, lower middle class functions of her day—as Luther knew them—at home and on her property, and did this independently, and not under the supervision of her husband. The routine of the husband of the house was coordinated with that of the wife and was not limited in regard to other household duties. Although the household is under the rule of the state its internal structure and the functions of its members among themselves follow an order that is unique to each household and is appropriate to the order of creation. The husband of the house, therefore, does not derive his authority from the state nor does he exercise it on behalf of the state. Within the household he is independent of the state.

The primary concern of the wife is economic. The husband, on the other hand, is primarily responsible for the religious aspect of family life. According to the preface of Luther's *Large Catechism*, he should go through the catechism with children and servants at least once a week.[19] He thus takes on the same function within his household as a pastor does in the parish. He is led by his spiritual care for his family appropriate to a catechetical instructor and receives this not by delegation from the church but through the position given him by God within the family as a baptized Christian.

The special function of the father is to be seen in that he cares for his children together with the mother. Children, therefore, stand in a similar relationship to their parents as do all people to God, who created them. The natural love for one's children, which arises from the biological connection to them, corresponds to the will of the creator. Yet this love dare not lead to a physical love for the parents rear their children for God and in God's stead. Hence parents should be just as concerned about the well-being of their children's souls as they are about the well-being of their bodies.

To bring up children for God does not mean, however, that they should be sent to a monastery. It means, rather, that they should be brought up so as to learn to serve in caring for others, in fulfillment of their vocation, in availability for their congregation, and under the authority of God. The stubbornness of a child who resists the authority of its parents is, according to Luther, the preliminary stage of the antisocial behavior of an adult and must be prevented through wise and if necessary strict discipline:

One should bring up children with great enthusiasm to have a healthy fear so that they fear those things for which one should have respect, but not so as to make them fearful, as many parents do, which hurts them throughout their life."[20]

Unnecessary severity toward children is therefore foolish because it very easily has the opposite effect as what was intended. It is also a sin against the nature of children who, in their simplicity, are nearer to the original condition of our first parents than are adults. Luther therefore reprimands parents who do not tolerate the natural childlikeness of their children or who are unwilling to recognize their individuality.

One sees in Luther's view of the relationship between parents and children a fundamental ethical relationship built upon mutual interaction. Also, one cannot accuse Luther of a patriarchal conception of the family in which the father is the unrestricted lord and master. This is true even though Luther assumes the priority of the husband over the wife in the family, which was the accepted family order during his lifetime. He based this view with tradition on the natural law. Luther's analogy between parents and secular authority is no longer functional for us, however, due to our democratically constituted government, even when we occasionally speak of a "father of the nation."

Although our historical distance to Luther becomes very clear in this chapter, we should not overlook the seemingly modern characteristics in his understanding of marriage and family. The rights of parents, for example, find their limits in the first commandment. And Luther himself went against the express will of his parents when he entered the monastery. Also, as can be seen in Luther's own marriage, a wife had a certain amount of freedom that was not subject to the rule of her husband. One could even speak here of a partnership marriage in the sense of an "intellectual and spiritual partnership of the wife,"[21] whereby husband and wife are dependent upon one another and are each concerned for the well-being of the other.

11

VOCATION

Luther's teaching concerning vocation has had an incredibly broad impact, extending well beyond the ecclesiastical and religious spheres. The combined influence of the Protestant church and the middle-class world of seventeenth and eighteenth century Germany produced an understanding of vocation as direct service to God. Vocation became the focal point of the human activities done in response to God's grace. Vocational loyalty was not just understood as loyalty to one's employer, but primarily as loyalty to God. In the periods of the Enlightenment and German Idealism in the late eighteenth and early nineteenth centuries, vocation ultimately became a fundamental concept in the ethical teaching about duty. Thus, according to the German philosopher Immanuel Kant (1724–1804), universal moral law is fulfilled in vocation. It is for this reason that Frederick the Great (1712–1786) who ruled Prussia as king from 1740 to 1786, proclaimed, "The prince is the first servant of his state." This description of vocation as duty rubbed off on the Prussian officials and government workers, who were known for their conscientious fulfillment of duty. Prussia's supremacy in Germany led to the development of an efficient and incorruptible bureaucracy that is still to this day exemplary in many ways.

For Luther, of course, such far-reaching ramifications were unintended. In his teaching about vocation, he was primarily concerned to dispel the view common in his time that priests and monks, through their vocation within a spiritual order, possessed a higher level of sanctification than those who had a secular vocation. In his 1521 writing, *On Monastic Vows*, Luther rejected the vocational privilege of monasticism, which held that monastics and priests had a vocational status superior to that of all others. From 1 Corinthians 7:20, "Let each of you remain in the condition in which you were called," Luther concludes that even an ordinary working person, without having to belong to a monastic order, can carry out here on earth an occupation that is good and commanded by God. For Luther, vocation no longer means to be called out of the world to a better and higher vocational status, but is seen rather as a calling to and within that place where one does his or her work.

Luther's rejection of the idea that a religious vocation is more worthy also follows from his conviction that all people are justified, that is to say accepted, through trust in God and not by being able to demonstrate certain good works before God. Because we have already received everything from God our creator, it would be a contradiction to want to be rewarded by God for one good work or another. Good works, therefore, have nothing to do with our justification: "Those things we do for God are not called good works, but what we should do for our neighbor, these are good works."[1] The fact that we perform good works here on earth is entirely motivated by the fact that our fellow human beings need our help. Those who perform some worldly task do it to the glory of God and as a service to their neighbor. One should even view the pastoral office from this perspective, because here, too, the service to one's neighbor and the glorification of God is expressed.

In our industrialized, urbanized society, however, this conception of vocation has largely disappeared. The modern understanding of one's "job" is characterized by maximizing investment and profit and by the ability to exercise control. But employers and employees today are increasingly taking notice of the fact that, without personal engagement, what is simply a job eventually amplifies the meaninglessness of life over the long run. Health problems, lack of motivation, and a decreasing quality of work are only some of the results. For more and more people, the level of remuneration and the shortness of the working week are no longer decisive, but what matters is the fact that the work is interesting, challenging, and personally engaging. So it is that Luther's emphasis on vocation as service of one's neighbor takes on renewed significance today. As we turn now to the task of briefly outlining Luther's understanding of vocation we must first view it in light of his understanding of one's status or station within society, which to some extent parallels his understanding of vocation.

SOCIETAL STATIONS

One cannot equate Luther's concept of *station* with the concept of class in the modern sense of the word. For Luther, one's station is first of all a general concept of order that makes it possible to group together all those people who in one way or another share something in common that distinguishes them from all others. In 1630 the hymn writer Johann Herrmann penned words that reflect the thought of Luther: "Give me the strength to do with ready heart and willing whatever you command, my calling here fulfilling."[2] Such a station could define a group (such a young girls), a social class (such as peasants), or a churchly estate (such as monks). Luther sees the various stations as standpoints for our actions. They are beyond our own arbitrary decisions, for the creator has established them and placed us within a particular station. These stations are places to which God calls us, so we can carry out a specific and unique vocation. Stations have a stabilizing function, but they cannot be compared to castes, which are closed in on themselves and do not allow any mobility from one station to another.

Tradition generally recognized three general stations: the teaching station, the economic station, and the political station. Luther accepted these on the whole, but he understood the economic station quite differently and described it as the station of family life.[3] Under the category of the station of the family, Luther understood first marriage, then the family in the narrower sense, that is, the community of parents and children, and also the family in the broader sense that includes domestic servants as well. Finally, Luther was able to classify the socio-economic and civic-societal relations of human beings under the category of the station of the family. Of importance for Luther in regard to this station is the economic relationships of people who all belong to the same social structure. For example, the union of husband and wife for the purpose of rearing children is also a biological necessity, as seen in the procurement of food and clothing. It is important in regard to activities within this station that the laws of life are not disregarded, thereby endangering the life of one's neighbor.

The political station, too, is established by God, for God desires order in society. Service in the state includes not only governing but also obeying. While the laws of biology (in the station of the family) are unchangeable, the laws that lie at the foundation of the political station are changeable. Here one finds appropriate to each era an order that binds people to one another. In the case of the teaching station, or churchly station, neither the laws of biology nor the laws of the state are applicable. We deal instead here with specific functions, so the teaching station has its own laws specific to itself.

Luther said, "God has prescribed a variety of stations in which one shall learn to live and to suffer—some in the marital, others in the spiritual, and still others in the station of government."[4] Yet none of these stations is higher than the others, and all have as their goal that they serve the other stations. To be sure, each person is placed within a specific station, but one can also change from one station to another, for instance from the spiritual station to the political or the economic. Yet every station has its own difficulties, so none is better or easier than the others. There is also no station in which there is no sin, for there is no station in which the command of God is fully carried out.

Why did God create and establish these stations in the first place? According to Luther's explanation, the stations embody the will of God, so God might provide for order and serve the needs of human beings through these external forms: "Without these masks [that is, stations], peace and discipline could not be preserved."[5] What is particularly important, once more to stress this point, is that none of these stations is placed above or below the others. Luther strictly rejected a higher status for the spiritual station, for there must not exist any hierarchy of stations. Each of the stations is equally necessary for human life. A station, then, is the objective range of duties connected to a particular position within society. The term *station*, however, is no way a synonym for *vocation*.

VOCATION AND CALLING

The word *vocation*, as we have indicated, is not another way of saying *station*. Vocation, to be sure, speaks of the same reality but from a different perspective. The stations are universally objective structures, while vocations are objective structures only when the individual is permanently connected with a particular one and is personally obligated to it. For instance, one is called to the pastoral office through human beings who represent God by exercising the church's right to call an individual. People are called to marriage because we are created, male or female, to rear children and establish a household. The biological perspective of the station of the family and the individual's personal decision become intertwined. Likewise, the station of a prince or a subject becomes a vocation inasmuch as a specific directive is given to a person to take up the tasks bound to this directive.

Vocation as divine service.

Belonging to a particular station does not automatically guarantee that carrying out the functions of that station will be "divine service," that is, that it will correspond to the divine will. If a person perceives that he or she has been called by God to a certain vocation, that person will be given the necessary assurance that this is his or her vocation, because a Christian does nothing without divine commission—without calling. It is a gift of God that we have one who has been given to us as neighbor, that we are subject to authorities, and that we have been placed in a family, for in these points of contact with other people, we are challenged to serve and to love. In this way we do the will of God and can view our work as divine service, regardless of its outwardly secular dimension.

Helping our neighbor, being a parent, and rearing children demonstrate a commonality in our calling whereby the differences between rich and poor and between those in authority and those under authority disappear:

> We should accustom ourselves to follow the order he [God] has prescribed for us. Whatever you may be, son, servant, or maid in the meanest circumstances, stay where you are, because you are in a station where God has put you.[6]

It is an important element of Luther's concept of vocation that every genuine vocation, being derived from divine calling, demands the engagement of the whole person. Luther continually warned that the preeminence of one station over another is reprehensible because it implies a contempt for the creator:

> We should remain there [in our vocation] with a happy conscience and know that through such work, more is accomplished than if one had made donations to every monastery and received every medal, even if it is the most menial chores.[7]

Thereby we are reminded of Luther's comment, "If everyone served his or her neighbor, then the whole world would be filled with divine service."[8]

Vocational mobility.

The question that must now be raised is whether the placement within a particular vocation or station is inescapably fixed. On one hand, Luther held firmly to the idea of unchangeable givens that place us within particular vocations. He argued, for instance, that a woman cannot become a man, a pig herder cannot become a lawyer, and a peasant is not qualified to be mayor.[9] Biological and educational differences allocate us to specific vocations. We are not only placed in a particular station but also in a particular vocation. Luther's view of stations and vocations remained within the framework of the societal structure of his time. He had to believe, therefore, that people were called into particular stations through their birth.

On the other hand, however, Luther in many ways broke through the idea that society is structured according to the stations into which people are born. He fought, for example, against the practice of barring those born out of wedlock from holding honorable vocations within the craft and trade professions. He also demanded the possibility for the advancement of children of common parents, but he did not, thereby, sanction the motive of increasing one's salary as justification for such advancement. Because every vocation is divine service, one cannot argue for a change in vocation on the basis of financial profit. Luther made parents vividly aware that through sufficient education, advancement to all government, educational, and ecclesiastical offices would be open to their children:

> It is not God's will that only those who are born kings, princes, lords, and nobles should exercise rule and lordship. He wills to have his beggars among them also, lest they think it is nobility of birth rather than God alone who makes lords and rulers.[10] . . . That is the way it will always be: your son and my son, that is, the children of the common people, will necessarily rule the world, both in the spiritual and the worldly estates.[11]

Advancement is open to all people who have the prerequisite educational qualifications. Luther therefore impressed on the territorial lords the great importance of the universities. He likewise wrote *To the Councilmen of All Cities in Germany That They Establish and Maintain Christian Schools*, as his writing of 1524 was titled. He demanded that basic educational opportunities be available to all people. Hence the children of poor parents were to be supported through governmental and ecclesiastical scholarships. Yet all the different possibilities of advancement are of no use if parents do not allow their children to take advantage of available educational opportunities. Parents, however, are also responsible to determine whether their children really have the necessary ability and interest to pursue higher education.

The fact that one has had a good education, however, does not automatically mean that he or she should demand to take up a more highly qualified vocation than what he or she would have had without this education. It does not, for example, do damage to a craftsperson, Luther contends, to have studied Latin just because it was an interesting subject, nor does it harm one to be well educated, whether or not one actually takes up the kind of position normally associated with the program of studies.[12] For Luther there are no ethical distinctions between the different vocations, and a fulfilling life is possible within each of them. If someone is unable to achieve much career advancement, he or she should not consider himself or herself deprived.

Only within certain limits can one choose one's own vocation, for the calling to a vocation always takes place through other people. Activity or training within a certain vocation always precedes the actual reception of a call into this vocation. Therefore, neither choosing a vocation nor carrying out its duties is a purely private matter. Luther frequently cautioned parents and teachers to keep in mind the well-being of the whole population when influencing a child regarding vocation. Important in regard to Luther's thoughts on vocation is a person's readiness to serve and to love:

> See to it first of all that you believe in Christ and are baptized. Afterward concern yourself with your vocation. I am called to be a pastor. Now when I preach, I perform a holy work pleasing to God. If you are a father or mother, believe in Jesus Christ and so you will be a holy father and a holy mother. Take watch over the early years of your children, let them pray, and discipline and spank them. Oversee the running of the household and the preparation of meals. Such things are nothing other than holy works, for you have been called to do them. That means they are your holy life and are a part of God's Word and your calling.[13]

This mutual serving that we encounter in the family and in marriage, as well as in the larger community, has already been shown to us in the service Christ. Humans are called to serve one another, just as Christ served us. Luther knew of no vocation that one could carry out without reference to the needs of the larger community. One is called when the community needs someone for a specific service and when one is qualified to meet the demands of this service. One cannot derive from this calling either an inappropriate pride in one's vocation or the absolute right to perform a particular vocation. A vocation is a service and can only be required when both the necessary qualifications in those who would serve in this vocation and the need for it in the community are present. Under these conditions, it is our duty not to forsake our vocation, even if it becomes too toilsome. If we have a genuine calling, then we dare not forsake our tasks but should stand courageously before them and accomplish them.

Luther's teaching on vocation is still able in our own day to help counter the individualistic and self-centered striving for one's own advantage, and to allow us to rediscover the fact that our work is meant to serve the common good. The world has changed decisively since Luther's world of the sixteenth century. Yet many basic problems addressed by Luther remain problems in our own time.

During the 450 years that separate us from Luther's time, tremendous changes have occurred in our world. We have witnessed an enormous explosion in our knowledge, and continuity with the past, which for Luther and his time was largely a matter of fact, has increasingly been called into question. We view as valid what we know now; what had meaning in the past seems unreliable. This break in tradition, which we can notice in all facets of life, contributes to an increasing sense of insecurity.

On the other hand, we have achieved in domesticating the world to a hitherto unknown extent. Martin Luther would only shake his head in disbelief if he were to see the technology we use in our leisure time, at the work place, in modern medicine, and in our household chores. Because of the domination of our environment, however, the world has been robbed of its divine connection, and it has become increasingly difficult to attribute to God any meaningful activity. Yet we have less difficulty acknowledging the work of destructive powers. Though many seemingly enlightened people no longer accept a personification of the evil one, the demonic is readily apparent in many parts of the world. We are reminded of its reality in the holocaust in Nazi Germany, in the self-destruction of the former Yugoslavia, and in the brutality of organized crime spawned by widespread poverty and greed. This means that the technological aspect of our world has changed our way of life in an unforeseen way.

But the fact that many of us live in fear and feel threatened in our daily existence has remained unchanged.

Confronted with the mercilessness and ambiguity of our world, the question of how to find a gracious God is not as antiquated as we might initially think. But Luther was not interested in a gracious God who would, like a good fairy, take all our anxieties away from us. Luther knew far too well that such a God would be a product of our desires and fantasies and would not be the living God, who in an unsurpassable way has shown himself to us in Jesus Christ. Therefore, Luther emphasized that the God who holds the whole world in his hand must also become the one who is the beginning, the center, and the goal of our life, if we want to overcome our insecurity and disorientation. To rediscover such a God some 2,000 years after Christ, and therefore to true faith in the true God, is a rewarding challenge for us. If Luther can give us some direction in this way, then the study of his theological focus is as contemporary today as it was 450 years ago.

Questions for Reflection

and Discussion

Chapter 1: Life and Work

1. Why was Martin Luther unable to find comfort in 1) Holy Communion, 2) penitence, or 3) the figure of Christ? How does Romans 1:16-17 help to explain Luther's struggle.

2. Luther sought to find a gracious God. What circumstances led Luther to focus on this concern? How would you describe the spiritual quest of people in the Western world today? What fuels this quest?

3. How did Luther understand "freedom of conscience"? Compare and contrast his understanding with that of people in Western culture today.

4. What were the concerns of the so-called enthusiasts, and how did they attempt to assert their views? What matters under dispute did Luther call *adiaphora*? How might the concept of adiaphora be helpful in the church today?

5. What were the issues involved in the peasant revolt? Outline Luther's counsel to both the princes and the peasants. Based on this counsel, how might Luther have responded to the concept of "civil disobedience"?

6. Summarize the issue of the real presence, on which Martin Luther and Huldreich Zwingli continued to disagree after the Marburg Colloquy. How is the issue of the real presence being addressed in Lutheran-Reformed dialogue today?

Chapter 2: The Correct Knowledge of God

1. What does Luther mean by "natural knowledge" of God? How does he believe people receive such knowledge?

2. According to Luther, why is natural knowledge of God inadequate? What is its greatest shortcoming? What would Luther say to New Age thinkers who believe we can find God within us?

3. Where does Luther say humans find God? What categories does Luther use to indicate that God comes to us but that we still experience God as mysterious? In what ways is God present to you? mysterious to you?

4. What does Luther mean by a "theology of the cross"?

Chapter 3: Faith and Reason

1. According to Luther, of what value is reason? To what realm does it belong? What are some questions that reason is unable to address.

2. According to Luther, because God gives all people reason, a sinful and godless person can be a good and upright ruler, parent, or businessperson. What limitations do all of us experience in our use of reason?

3. How does Luther define faith? How is faith different from belief? What implications does this difference have for our understanding of the claim that we are saved by faith?

4. What is the relationship between faith and the Word of God? Why is it impossible for us to make a decision to have faith? Do you regard this impossibility as bad new or good news? Why?

5. If everyone must believe for himself or herself, what is the role of the community in our relationship with God? What does this say about the responsibility of individuals to invite others into their Christian faith communities?

6. What is the relationship between faith and seeing and knowing? Does this relationship cause any conflicts for you, for example, in regard to the origin of the universe? life after death? other matters?

7. Luther believed faith and experience belong together. In what ways does your experience support your faith? How does experience challenge your faith?

8. Why does Luther say faith comes before the experience of God? How can the tension between faith and experience be resolved?

Chapter 4: The Divinity of God

1. Why is Luther so insistent that "God is from first to last the deciding force in the matter of human salvation"? What would it mean for us if Luther were wrong?

2. What problems arise when we emphasize the sole-activity of God? Why weren't these issues problematic for Luther?

3. Luther denies that entrusting everything to God requires us to switch off our reason. Do you agree or disagree? Why?

4. What difference would it make for you if God were an impersonal fate, rather than a personal being? Would that change the way you relate to other people? Would you view the future differently?

5. What is the relationship between God's power and our effort? What does this mean for the way we conduct ourselves in our families? at work? at the ballot box?

6. What is our proper response to God's goodness to us?

Chapter 5: Humanity between God and Satan

1. How does Luther describe the devil? When you think of the presence of evil in the world, do you think of a personal being like the devil, or an impersonal force? How might your understanding of evil change if you held the opposite view?

2. Luther says we are always under the power of either God or Satan. Luther also says we are at the same time saint and sinner (*simul justus et peccator*). How do you reconcile these seemingly contradictory statements?

3. For what purposes, according to Luther, does God use evil? How does the notion that God uses evil affect your perception of God as a loving God?

4. According to the author, Luther believes "tribulation . . . always has two faces: the face of God and the face of the devil." What examples from your own life describe the two faces of tribulation.

5. The author says what is negative in this world is always ambiguous and may be understood "as the just results of our estranged existence from God" or "as the outcome of a chaotic activity." Do both explanations apply to a single event, such as an earthquake or a murder? Does human responsibility play a role in either explanation? Why or why not?

Chapter 6: The Ordering Activity of God (The Two Kingdoms)

1. Describe St. Augustine's and Luther's understanding of the two kingdoms. How were their views similar? dissimilar? Why was Luther not able to follow Augustine's thinking?

2. Some argue that, relative to the world, the church today is in a position more akin to the church in Augustine's time than Luther's. Is Augustine's or Luther's understanding of the two kingdoms more useful for the church today? Why?

3. In what sense are the two kingdoms unified? What implications does this have for the role of Christians in politics?

4. The author says Luther believes it is not Christ but rather the law of each particular nation that answers the social and cultural questions concerning what a parent, teacher, politician, or judge should do in certain situations. How might Luther respond to the notion of a "Christian counselor" or "Christian parenting"? According to Luther, what difference, if any, might there be between a Christian counselor and a non-Christian counselor, or a Christian parent and a non-Christian parent?

5. What criticisms have been leveled against Luther's understanding of the two kingdoms?

6. In what ways is Luther's doctrine of the two kingdoms important for us today?

7. Some Christians believe it is their duty to try to influence the political process. Other Christians are heard to say something akin to, "Pastor, I love your sermons. Just be sure to keep politics out of the pulpit." What implications does Luther's thinking on the two kingdoms have for these two groups?

Chapter 7: Scripture Alone

1. How was Luther's translation of the Bible different from translations into German done before his? Why did Luther think it was so important to prepare this translation?
2. What four methods of interpreting Scripture were common in Luther's time? What principles of interpretation did Luther put forth? What are the strengths and limitations of these principles? Which, if any, of these principles are useful for biblical interpretation today?
3. Luther insisted there is a canon within the canon. What evidence is there that he used historical criticism in his study of Scripture? What standard or boundaries did Luther apply to this criticism? To what extent can or should this standard be applied today?
4. Describe Luther's understanding of the relationship between the Old and New Testaments, and between the Old Testament and Christ. In what sense is the Old Testament binding or relevant for non-Jews? In what sense is it not binding?
5. How does Luther's "spiritual interpretation" of the Old Testament differ from allegorical interpretations? Can we interpret Scripture using only Luther's principles? Why or why not?

Chapter 8: Law and Gospel

1. What is the relationship of the Ten Commandments to natural law? What is the content of "the law"?
2. Briefly explain the two uses of the law, as delineated by Luther. Why did Luther disagree with the Antinomians, who argued that we only need the law in the civil arena? How does the distinction between the two uses of the law address the separation of church and state in the United States?
3. Why do we need both law and gospel? How might law and gospel be confused? What effect might the confusion of law and gospel have on an individual's relationship with God?
4. Luther believes "that law and gospel have two distinct and contrary functions, but both are functions of the same Word of God and occur simultaneously." Give an example of how the same word can be heard as both law and gospel.

5. What is meant by the third use of the law? Why does Luther say there is no third use? If there were a third use of the law, how would that affect other basic doctrines, particularly *sola fide*, by faith alone?

Chapter 9: Church and Sacrament

1. What are the distinguishing marks of the church? What is the role of the church in salvation? Would Luther ascribe to the idea of universal salvation? Why or why not?
2. How did Luther's understanding of "saints" differ from the view prevalent in his day? Of what value are the "traditional" saints to Christians today?
3. According to Luther, what does it mean to be the "communion of saints"? How have you experienced the communion of saints as a gift? How have you experienced it as an obligation? How is the communion of saints different from other communities?
4. In what ways are Christians called to be priests for one another? When was a time you were aware you were exercising your priesthood. When was a time when another (nonordained) Christian was a priest to you.
5. According to Luther, what are the foundations of the preaching office? What is the relationship of the pastor to the congregation? Who properly calls a person to be a pastor?
6. How does Luther understand the role of tradition in the ordering of the church? How does his understanding differ from the Anabaptists'? What is the relationship of tradition to Scripture?
7. What is the source of Scripture's authority? What implications does this understanding of the authority of Scripture have for the idea that Scripture is infallible and to be read literally?
8. According to Luther, what is a sacrament? Compare this definition with those of the Roman and Reformed traditions.
9. What is the relationship between baptism and repentance? On what basis does Luther insist on the validity of infant baptism?
10. What does Luther mean by the "real presence"? Why is the real presence of Christ's body and blood in Holy Communion important for individual Christians?

Chapter 10: Love, Marriage, and Parenthood

1. According to Luther, how does original sin affect marriage and sexuality?
2. In Luther's mind, what is the purpose of marriage? What role does marriage play relative to the rest of creation? How does celibacy fit into the picture?
3. In what sense is marriage a holy estate, and in what sense is it part of the

secular order? What implications might this distinction have for the role of clergy in weddings in the United States today?

4. What does Luther say marriage means for the husband and wife? What is its significance for child rearing? How does the family structure Luther describes compare to the structure of the family you grew up in? the structures of families you are familiar with now?

5. According to Luther, what is the basis for the relationship between parents and children? Again, how does this relationship compare to the relationship you had with your own parents? the relationships between parents and children you are familiar with now?

Chapter 11: Vocation

1. What was Luther's primary concern regarding vocation? What was the basis for his understanding of vocation? Compare and contrast your understanding of vocation, job, and service with Luther's understanding of these areas.

2. What stations were recognized by tradition in Luther's day? How did Luther's views differ from tradition's? What function do stations serve in the created order?

3. What is the difference between a station and a vocation? What does it mean that vocation is "divine service"? How does the concept of divine service affect your view of your own vocation?

4. What was Luther's understanding of vocational mobility. How might Luther's thoughts on this matter be helpful to employees in the U.S. job market today?

5. Which of Luther's ideas has had the greatest impact on your understanding of your relationship to God? your relationship to other members of your faith community? your relationship to your family?

SELECTED BIBLIOGRAPHY

General Works on the Reformation

Bainton, Roland. *The Reformation of the Sixteenth Century*. Boston: Beacon Press, 1952, 1985.

Chadwick, Owen. *The Reformation. (Pelican History of the Church Series)*. New York: Penguin Books, 1964.

Ozment, Steven. *The Age of Reform, 1250–1550: An Intellectual and Religious History of Late Medieval and Reformation Europe*. New Haven: Yale University Press, 1980.

_____. *Protestants: The Birth of a Revolution*. New York: Doubleday and Co., Inc., 1992.

Pelikan, Jaroslav. *The Christian Tradition: A History of the Development of Doctrine. Reformation of Church and Dogma (1300–1700)*, vol. 4. Chicago: University of Chicago Press, 1984.

Spitz, Lewis W. *The Protestant Reformation, 1517–1559. (The Rise of Modern Europe Series)*. New York: Harper & Row, 1985.

_____. *Renaissance and Reformation*. 2 vols. St. Louis: Concordia Publishing House, 1971, 1980.

Luther's Life and Theology

Althaus, Paul. *The Ethics of Martin Luther*. Translated by Robert Schultz. Philadelphia: Fortress Press, 1972.

_____. *The Theology of Martin Luther*. Translated by Robert Schultz. Philadelphia: Fortress Press, 1966.

Altmann, Walter. *Luther and Liberation: A Latin American Perspective*. Translated by Mary M. Solberg. Minneapolis: Augsburg Fortress, 1992.

Aulén, Gustaf. *Christus Victor*. Translated by A. G. Hebert. New York: Macmillan, 1969.

Bainton, Roland H. *Here I Stand: A Life of Martin Luther*. Nashville: Abingdon, 1950, 1978.

Bornkamm, Heinrich. *Luther's World of Thought*. Translated by Martin H. Bertram. St. Louis: Concordia Publishing House, 1958.

Brecht, Martin. *Martin Luther: His Road to Reformation, 1483–1521*. Translated by James L. Schaaf. Philadelphia: Fortress Press, 1985.

_____. *Martin Luther: Shaping and Defining the Reformation, 1521–1532*. Translated by James L. Schaaf. Minneapolis: Fortress Press, 1990.

_____. *Martin Luther: The Preservation of the Church, 1532–1546*. Translated by James L. Schaaf. Minneapolis: Fortress Press, 1992.

Ebeling, Gerhard. *Luther: An Introduction to His Thought.* Translated by R. A. Wilson. Philadelphia: Fortress Press, 1970.

Edwards, Mark U. *Luther and the False Brethren.* Stanford: Stanford University Press, 1975.

_____. *Luther's Last Battles: Politics and Polemics, 1531-1546.* Ithaca, N.Y.: Cornell University Press, 1983.

Elert, Werner. *The Structure of Lutheranism: The Theology and Philosophy of Life of Lutheranism, 16th and 17th Centuries,* vol. 1. Translated by Walter Hansen. St. Louis: Concordia Publishing House, 1962, 1974.

Erikson, Erik H. *Young Man Luther.* New York: W. W. Norton and Co., Inc., 1962.

Forde, Gerhard O. *Where God Meets Man: Luther's Down-to-Earth Approach to the Gospel.* Minneapolis: Augsburg Publishing House, 1972.

Forell, George W. *Faith Active in Love: An Investigation of the Principles Underlying Luther's Social Ethics.* Minneapolis: Augsburg Publishing House, 1954.

Gerrish, Brian. *Grace and Reason: A Study in the Theology of Martin Luther.* Oxford: Oxford University Press, 1962.

Grane, Leif. *The Augsburg Confession: A Commentary.* Translated by John Rasmussen. Minneapolis: Augsburg Publishing House, 1987.

Gritsch, Eric W. *Martin—God's Court Jester: Luther in Retrospect.* Philadelphia: Fortress Press, 1983.

Gritsch, Eric W., and Robert W. Jenson. *Lutheranism: The Theological Movement and Its Confessional Writings.* Philadelphia: Fortress Press, 1976.

Haile, H. G. *Luther: An Experiment in Biography.* Garden City, N.Y.: Doubleday and Co., Inc., 1980.

Kittelson, James M. *Luther the Reformer: The Story of the Man and His Career.* Minneapolis: Augsburg Publishing House, 1987.

Lienhard, Marc. *Luther: Witness to Jesus Christ.* Translated by Edwin H. Robinson. Minneapolis: Augsburg Publishing House, 1982.

Loeschen, John R. *Wrestling with Luther: An Introduction to the Study of His Thought.* St. Louis: Concordia Publishing House, 1976.

Loewenich, Walther von. *Luther's Theology of the Cross.* Translated by J. A. Bouman. Minneapolis: Augsburg Publishing House, 1976.

_____. *Martin Luther: The Man and His Work.* Translated by Lawrence Denef. Minneapolis: Augsburg Publishing House, 1986.

Lohse, Berhard. Martin Luther: *An Introduction to His Life and Work.* Translated by Robert C. Schultz. Philadelphia: Fortress Press, 1986.

McGrath, Alister E. *Luther's Theology of the Cross: Martin Luther on Justification, 1509-1519.* New York/London: Basil Blackwell, 1985.

Oberman, Heiko A. *Luther: Man Between God and the Devil.* Translated by Eileen Walliser-Schwarzbart. New Haven: Yale University Press, 1986.

Olivier, Daniel. *Luther's Faith: The Cause of the Gospel in the Church.* Translated by John Tonkin. St. Louis: Concordia Publishing House, 1982.

_____. *The Trial of Luther.* Translated by John Tonkin. St. Louis: Concordia Publishing House, 1979.

Pelikan, Jaroslav. *Obedient Rebels: Catholic Substance and Protestant Principle in Luther's Reformation*. New York: Harper & Row, 1964.

_____. *Spirit vs. Structure: Luther and the Institutions of the Church*. New York: Harper and Row, 1968.

Prenter, Regin. *Spiritus Creator*. Translated by John M. Jensen. Philadelphia: Muhlenberg Press, 1953.

Rupp, E. Gordon. *Luther's Progress to the Diet of Worms*. Chicago: Wilcox and Follet, 1951.

_____. *The Righteousness of God: Luther Studies*. 3rd ed. London: Hodder and Stoughton, 1968.

Selected Writings of Luther

Lull, Timothy F., ed. *Martin Luther's Basic Theological Writings*. Minneapolis: Fortress Press, 1989.

Luther, Martin. *Kritische Gesamtausgabe*. Weimar: Hermann Böhlaus Nachfolger, 1883.

_____. *Luther's Works, American Edition*. 56 vols. Edited by Jaroslav Pelikan and Helmut T. Lehmann. St. Louis: Concordia Publishing House; and Philadelphia: Fortress Press, 1955–1967.

Maurer, Wilhelm. *Historical Commentary on the Augsburg Confession*. Translated by H. George Anderson. Philadelphia: Fortress Press, 1986.

Tappert, Theodore, ed. and trans. *The Book of Concord: The Confessions of the Evangelical Lutheran Church*. Philadelphia: Fortress Press, 1959.

Notes

Works frequently cited in the notes have been identified by the following abbreviations:

BC   *The Book of Concord*. (Philadelphia, 1959).

LW   *Luther's Works, American Edition*. (Philadelphia and St.Louis, 1955-1967).

WA   D. *Martin Luthers Werke*. Kritische Gesamtausgabe. (Weimar, 1883).

WA BR   D. *Martin Luthers Werke*. Briefwechsel. (Weimar, 1930).

WA TR   D. *Martin Luthers Werke*. Tischreden. (Weimar, 1912-1921).

Chapter 1: Life and Work

1. Luther, "Tischrede" no. 6250 (undated), in *WA TR* 5,558.13f.
2. Luther, "Table Talk" no. 2888a (1533), in *LW* 54:178.
3. Walther von Loewenich, *Martin Luther: Der Mann und das Werk* (Munich: List, 1982), 42; and Luther, *In epistolam S. Pauli ad Galatas Commentarius* (1535), in *WA* 40 I,531.24f.
4. Luther, Eine Predigt, *wie man Kinder zu Schulen halten solle*, in *WA* 30,576.13.
5. Cited in Otto Scheel, *Martin Luther: Vom Katholizismus zur Reformation*, vol. 1 (Tübingen: J. C. B. Mohr (Paul Siebeck), 1917), 296, note 66, from a letter written in Bamberg in April 1520.
6. Luther, "Tischrede" no. 4707 (1539), in *WA TR* 4,440.9f.
7. Ibid., *WA TR* 4,440.11-17.
8. According to Martin Luther, commenting on Matthew 21:12, Matthew 18-24 in *Predigten ausgelegt* (1537-1540), in *WA* 47, 379.9f.
9. Luther, "Table Talk" no. 3556 A (1537), in *LW* 54:234.
10. Luther, comment on Romans 1:17: Lectures on Romans (1515/1516), in *LW* 25:151. The German text here does not refer to the righteousness by which God is righteousness in himself but rather the righteousness through which one becomes righteous in himself or herself. So we read: "Und hier darf wieder unter 'Gerechtigkeit Gottes' nicht die verstanden werden, durch die einer in sich selbst gerecht ist, sondern durch die wir von ihm selbst gerecht gemacht werden . . ." in *WA* 56,172.3ff.
11. Luther, "Letter to John Lang. Wittenberg, May 18, 1517" in *LW* 48:41f.
12. Friedrich Myconius, *Geschichte der Reformation* (1517-1542), ed. Otto Clemen (Leipzig: Boigtländer's Quellenbücher, 1914), 22.
13. Cited in Nikolaus Paulus, Johann Tetzel, *der Ablaßprediger* (Mainz: Franz Kirchheim, 1899), 139.
14. Luther, "Preface to the Complete Edition of Luther's Latin Writings" (1545) in *LW* 34:335f.
15. Duke George in a letter from October 1520 to "Dr. Johannes Hennigh, dean of Meißen, currently in Rome," (no. 175), in *Akten und Briefe zur Religionspolitik Herzog Georgs von Sachsen*, vol. 1: 1517-1524, ed. Felician Geß (Leipzig: B. G. Teubner, 1905), 139.

16. Luther, "Table Talk" no. 131 (November/December 1531), in *LW* 54:19.

17. "Luther at the Diet of Worms," in *LW* 32:112f.

18. Cited by Irmgard Höß, Georg Spalatin. *1484-1545: Ein Leben in der Zeit des Humanismus und der Reformation* (Weimar: Hermann Böhlaus Nachfolger, 1956), 197.

19. The dispatch of Aleander "to the Vice Chancellor Medici" on April 29, 1521, printed in Theodor Brieger, *Quellen und Forschungen zur Geschichte der Reformation*, vol. 1 (Gotha: Friedrich Andreas Perthes, 1884), 170.

20. From a letter of Elector Frederick of Saxony to Duke Johann of Saxony (April 14, 1525), printed in. Carl Eduard Förstemann, *Neues Urkundenbuch zur Geschichte der evangelischen Kirchen-Reformation* (Hamburg: Friedrich Andreas Perthes, 1842), 259 (Reprint: Hildesheim/New York, 1976).

21. Luther, "Letter to Johann Rühel. Seeburg, May 4, 1525," in *LW* 49:111.

22. Luther, "Letter to Nicholas von Amsdorf. Wittenberg, June 21, 1525," in *LW* 49:117.

23. Luther, "Tischrede" no. 129 (November/December 1531), in *WA TR* 1,53.27f.

24. Luther, "Letter to Elector John. Coburg, May 15, 1530," in *LW* 49:297f.

25. Luther, "Letter to Weneslaus Link in Nuremburg. January 15, 1531," (Nr. 1772), in *WA BR* 6,16.14ff.

26. Luther, "Letter to Mrs. Martin Luther. Eisleben, February 1, 1546," in *LW* 50:290ff.

27. For this and the following quote cf. the report of Justus Jonas from February 18, 1546, printed in Christof Schubart, *Die Berichte über Luthers Tod und Begräbnis* (Weimar: Böhlau, 1917), 5 and 9.

28. Luther, "Table Talk" no. 6975 (February 16, 1546), in *WA TR* 6,303.12ff.

Chapter 2: The Correct Knowledge of God

1. Luther, *Lectures on Galatians* (1535), in *LW* 26:399.

2. Luther, *The Large Catechism*, in *The Book of Concord*, 365.

3. Luther on Deuteronomy 5:6, *Predigten über das 5. Buch Mose* (1529), in *WA* 28,609.29–610.19.

4. Luther, in his exposition of Jonah 1:5, *Lectures on Jonah* (1526), in *LW* 19:54.

5. Ibid., *LW* 19:53. *The Epicureans*, named after Greek philosopher Epicurus (ca. 341-270 B.C.) were known for their fearlessness before the gods and their pursuit of happiness.

6. Luther, commenting on Romans 1:19, *Commentary on the Epistle to the Romans*, trans. J. T. Mueller (Grand Rapids: Kregel, 1976), 43.

7. Luther, on Genesis 17:7, *Lectures on Genesis* (1535-1545), in *LW* 3:117.

8. Luther, *Über das 1. Buch Mose. Predigten* (1527), in *WA* 24,9.20f.

9. Luther, expounding upon the first commandment in *The Large Catechism*, 367.

10. Luther, *Lectures on Galatians*, 399.

11. Luther, on John 1:18, *Auslegungen des ersten und zweiten Kapitels Johannes in Predigten* (1517/1538), in *WA* 46,667.10f.

12. Luther, *Against the Heavenly Prophets in the Matter of Images and Sacraments* (1525), in *LW* 40:96f.

13. Luther, "Epistel am Sonntag Trinitatis. Röm 11,33-36," *Crucigers Sommerpostille* (1537), in *WA* 21,510.39-511.1.

14. Luther, on Jonah 1:5, *Lectures on Jonah* (1526), in *LW* 19:53.

15. Luther, "Tischrede," no. 6530 (undated), in *WA TR* 6,20.19-29.

16. Luther, *Eine kurze Form der zehn Gebote, des Glaubens und des Vaterunsers* (1520), in *WA* 7,205.17.

17. Luther, on Genesis 43:23, *Lectures on Genesis* (1535-1545): *LW* 7:336.
18. Luther, on Jonah 1:4, *Lectures on Jonah*, Latin text (1525), in *LW* 19:11.
19. Luther, in a sermon from September 10, 1525, on Luke 17:11ff., in *WA* 17 I,412.19f.
20. Luther, on Jonah 1:4, *Lectures on Jonah*, Latin text (1525), in *LW* 19:11.
21. Luther, on Romans 1:19, *Lectures on Romans* (1515/1516), in *LW* 25:157.
22. Luther, on Isaiah 65:1: *Vorlesung über Jesaia* (1527-1529), in *WA* 25,383.10f.
23. Luther, *Sermon von dem Sakrament* (1526), in *WA* 19,492.22-26.
24. Luther, *Predigten über das 5. Buch Mose* (1529), in *WA* 28,608.8f.
25. Luther, in a scholia of 1534 on Isaaiah 4: *Vorlesungen über Jesaia* (1527-1529), in *WA* 25,106.43f.
26. Luther, commenting on Jonah 1:5, *Lectures on Jonah* (1526), in *LW* 19:55.
27. Luther, in a sermon on Genesis 11: *Predigten über das erste Buch Mose* (1523/1524), in *WA* 14,213.13.
28. Luther, "Table Talk" no. 153, in *LW* 54:22.
29. Luther, commenting on Hebrews 1:2, *Lectures on Hebrews* (1517), in *LW* 29:111.
30. Luther, in his explanation of Psalm 25: *Dictata super Psalterium* (1513-1516), in *WA* 3,143.9f.
31. Luther, in his explanation of Psalm 5:12: *Operationes in Psalmos* (1519-1521), in *WA* 5,176.32f.
32. Luther, in his explanation of thesis 20 of the *Heidelberg Disputation*, in *LW* 31:53.
33. Ibid., on thesis 21, *LW* 31:53.
34. See Luther in his exposition of Psalm 90:7, *Enarratio Psalmi XC* (1534/1535), in *WA* 40 III,543.1f.
35. Luther in his explanation of thesis 6 of the *Heidelberg Disputation*, in *LW* 31:45.

Chapter 3: Faith and Reason

1. Luther, in a sermon on Judica Sunday on John 8:46-59, *Fastenpostille 1525*, in *WA* 17/2,235.17-20.
2. Luther, *The Small Catechism*, in *Book of Concord*, ed. T. Tappert, 345.
3. Luther, *The Disputation Concerning Man* (1536), in *LW* 34:137.
4. Luther, on Exodus 13:11-13, *Predigten über das 2. Buch Mose* (1524-1527), in *WA* 16,261.29-32.
5. Luther, in a sermon on Isaiah 60:1-6, *Kirchenpostille* (1522), in *WA* 10 I 1,531.6-16.
6. Luther, in a sermon on John 1:1-14, *Kirchenpostille* (1522), in *WA* 10 I 1,191.14ff.
7. Luther in his sermon from December 21, 1536, in Lichtenberg, *Predigten des Jahres 1536*, in *WA* 41,736.23-737.9, where he clearly speaks about how limited reason is in its knowledge of the work of God.
8. Luther, commenting on Psalm 33, *Dictata super Psalterium* (1513-16), in *WA* 3,180.26; and in *The Sacrament of Penance* (1519), in *LW* 35:16.
9. Luther, in a sermon on Matthew 21:1-9, *Adventpostille* (1525), in *WA* 10 I 2,24.2-13.
10. Luther, *The Small Catechism*, in *The Book of Concord*, 344f.
11. Ibid., 345.
12. Luther, *Commentary on Romans*, trans. J. T. Mueller (Grand Rapids: Kregel, 1976), xvif.
13. Luther, in a sermon on Matthew 7:15ff., *Predigten des Jahres 1522*, in *WA* 10 III,259.13-18.
14. Luther, in a sermon on Mark 8:1ff., *Predigten des Jahres 1528*, in *WA* 27,276.8f.
15. Luther, *Sermons on the Gospel of St. John* (1537), in *LW* 24:151.
16. Luther, in a sermon on Mark 16:1-8, *Sommerpostille* (1526), in *WA* 10 I 2,223.6ff.

Chapter 4: The Divinity of God

1. Luther, *The Bondage of the Will* (1525), in *LW* 33:38.
2. Ibid., *LW* 33:155.
3. Luther on Genesis 27, In *Genesin Declamationes* (1527), in *WA* 24,476.4.
4. See Luther, *Predigten über das 2. Buch Mose* (1524-1527), in *WA* 16,141.3-6.
5. Heinz Zahrnt, *Luther deutet Geschichte: Erfolg und Mißerfolg im Licht des Evangeliums* (Munich: P. Müller, 1952), 190.
6. Luther in a sermon on Romans 11:33-36, *Crucigers Sommerpostille* (1526), in *WA* 21,521.21-25.
7. Luther, *That These Words of Christ*, "This Is My Body," etc., *Still Stand Firm Against the Fanatics* (1527), in *LW* 37:58.
8. Luther in a sermon on Matthew 4:1ff.: *Fastenpostille* (1525), in *WA* 17, 192.28ff.
9. Luther, *The Small Catechism*, in *The Book of Concord*, 347.
10. Luther in his explanation of the First Commandment in *The Large Catechism*: in *The Book of Concord*, 368.
11. Luther, "Psalm 147," (1532), in *LW* 14:124.
12. Luther, *Lectures on Jonah* (1526), in *LW* 19:68.
13. Luther, *The Bondage of the Will* (1525), in *LW* 33:176.
14. Luther in his exposition of Psalm 51:16 (1532), in *LW* 12:397.

Chapter 5: Humanity between God and Satan

1. Luther in a sermon on St. Michael's day: *Predigten des Jahres 1531*, in *WA* 34 , 264.16.
2. Luther in his exposition of Genesis 28,12ff., *Lectures on Genesis* (1535-1545), in *LW* 5:221.
3. Luther in his exposition of Galatians 4:29: In *epistolam S. Pauli ad Galatas Commentarius* (1535), in *WA* 40I, 678.26 [*LW* 26:455]; and in his sermon on St. Michael's day, *WA* 34 , 232.28-233.16.
4. *Lutheran Book of Worship*, hymn no. 228.
5. See Luther, *That These Words of Christ*, "This Is My Body," etc., *Still Stand Firm Against the Fanatics* (1527), in *LW* 37:17.
6. Luther in his exposition of Matthew 12:30: *Annotationes in aliquot capita Matthaei* (1527), in *WA* 38,545.28f.
7. Luther, *The Bondage of the Will* (1525), in *LW* 33:65f.
8. Luther, *That These Words of Christ*, "This Is My Body," etc., *Still Stand Firm Against the Fanatics* (1527), in *LW* 37:17.
9. Luther in his exposition of Psalm 90:3: *Ennaratio Psalmi XC* (1534/35), in *WA* 40 III, 516.25-517.14; 518.11f.; 519.13f.
10. Luther in his explanation of Genesis 4:8: *Lectures on Genesis* (1535-45), in *LW* 1:273; and in a sermon from 20 May 1532: *Predigten des Jahres* 1532, in *WA* 36,180.17.
11. Luther in a sermon on Dtn. 4:29ff., *Predigten über das 5. Buch Mose* (1529), in *WA* 28,578.21ff.
12. Luther on Psalm 51:4 (1532) in *LW* 12:346f.
13. Luther, commenting on Genesis 32:1f., *Lectures on Genesis* (1535-1545), in *LW* 6:90.
14. Luther in a sermon on Matthew 18:1ff., *Predigten des Jahres 1531*, in *WA* 34 , 240.25f.
15. Luther, *Predigten über das 2. Buch Mose* (1524-1527), in *WA* 16,143.4f.
16. Luther on Psalm 51:8 (1532) in *LW* 12:373.

Chapter 6: The Ordering Activity of God (The Two Kingdoms)

1. Luther, *Explanations of the Ninety-five Theses* (1518), in *LW* 31:244.
2. Luther on Zech. 1:7, *Lectures on Zechariah* (1527), in *LW* 20:173.
3. Luther, *Whether Soldiers, Too, Can Be Saved* (1526), in *LW* 46:99f.
4. Luther on Zech. 1:7, in *LW* 20:172.
5. Luther, *Die Zirkulardisputation über Matthew 19,21* (1539), thesis 52, in *WA* 39 , 42.3f.
6. Luther in a sermon on Matthew 5:38-42, *Wochenpredigen über Matthew 5-7* (1530-32), in *WA* 32,390.15-18.
7. Luther, *Temporal Authority: To What Extent it Should be Obeyed* (1523), in *LW* 45:113.
8. See the illustration given by Luther in a sermon on Matthew 5:1ff., *Wochenpredigten über Matthew 5-7* (1530-32), in *WA* 32,304.21-32.
9. See Luther's distinction between the worldly and spiritual regiments along with all the examples which he provides in his explanation of Zechariah 1:7, *Lectures on Zechariah* (1527), in *LW* 20:172.
10. Luther, *Temporal Authority*, in *LW* 45:104f.
11. Luther in a sermon on Luke 16:1ff. from August 17, 1522, *Predigten des Jahres 1522*, in *WA* 10III, 275.7-10.
12. Luther, *Temporal Authority*, in *LW* 45:126.
13. Luther, *Admonition to Peace, A Reply to the Twelve Articles of the Peasants in Swabia* (1525), *LW* 46:22f.
14. Ibid., 46:25.
15. Ibid., 46:40.
16. Luther, *Against the Robbing and Murdering Hordes of Peasants* (1525), *LW* 46:52f.
17. Luther, *Temporal Authority*, in *LW* 45:124f.
18. Luther, *Den 82. Psalm ausgelegt* (1530), in *WA* 31I,193,24f.
19. Luther, *Temporal Authority*, in *LW* 45:91.

Chapter 7: Scripture Alone

1. Luther, "Table Talk" no. 2790a (1532), in *WA TR* 2,661,16ff.
2. Luther, *De potestate leges forendi in ecclesia* (1530), in *WA* 30 ,687.32f.
3. Luther, in a sermon from July 25, 1522, *Predigten des Jahres 1522*, in *WA* 10 III,238.10f.
4. Luther, in his preface to his exposition of I Peter, *Sermons on the First Epistle of St. Peter* (1523), in *LW* 30:3.
5. Luther, "Preface to the Epistles of St. James and St. Jude" (1522), in *LW* 35:396.
6. Ibid.
7. Ibid., 357ff.
8. Ibid., 399ff.
9. Luther, "Evangelium in der hohen Christmesse. Joh. 1,1-14," *Kirchenpostille* 1522, in *WA* 10 I 1,181.15-22.
10. Luther, *Preface to the Old Testament* (1523), in *LW* 35:236.
11. Luther, on Exodus 19f., *Predigten über das 2. Buch Mose* (1524-1527), in *WA* 16,378.9. The Sachsenspiegel was an influential and well-known code of Saxon economic and social laws compiled by Eike von Repgow in the early thirteenth century.
12. Ibid., *WA* 16,385.7ff.

13. Luther, *Against the Heavenly Prophets in the Matter of Images and Sacraments* (1525), in *LW* 40:92.
14. Ibid., *LW* 40:98.
15. Luther, *Sermons on the First Epistle of St. Peter* (1523), in *LW* 30:19.
16. See Luther, *Preface to the Old Testament*, in *LW* 35:247f.
17. See Luther, Der 111. *Psalm ausgelegt* (1530), in *WA* 31 I,396f.

Chapter 8: Law and Gospel

1. Philipp Melanchthon, *Apology of the Augsburg Confession* (1530) IV, in *The Book of Concord*, 107ff., who expresses the view of Luther.
2. See Luther, *Die Thesen gegen die Antinomer* (1537-1540), in *WA* 39 I,344.30 where he cites the theses of the Antinomians which he responds to with his own series of theses; cf. especially *WA* 39 I,349.39f.
3. Luther, In *epistolam Pauli ad Galatas commentarius* (1519), in *WA* 2,466.12f.
4. See Luther, *Die Promotionsdisputation von Palladius und Tilemann* (1537), thesis 36, in *WA* 39 I,219.23f.
5. Luther, "Die dritte Disputation gegen die Antinomer" (1538): *Die Thesen gegen die Antinomer* (1537-1540), in *WA* 39 I,546.14ff.
6. Ibid., thesis 17, in *WA* 39 I,351.1f.
7. Luther in his explanation of baptism in *The Small Catechism*, in *The Book of Concord*, 349.
8. Luther, "Die erste Disputation gegen die Antinomer," in *WA* 39 I,398.15f.
9. Luther, *Thesen de fide* (1535), in *WA* 39 I,47.25-36.
10. Here the distinction made by Paul Althaus between law and commandment in: *The Theology of Martin Luther*, trans. R. Schultz (Philadelphia: Fortress Press, [1966] 1989), 271ff.

Chapter 9: Church and Sacrament

1. Luther, *Ad Librum eximii Magistri Nostri Magistri Ambrosii Catharini, defensoris Silvestri Prieritatis acerrimi, responsio* (1520), in: *WA* 7,720.36ff.
2. Luther, *Eine kurze Form der zehn Gebote, eine kurze Form des Glaubens, eine kurze Form des Vaterunsers* (1520), in: *WA* 7,219.6ff.
3. Luther, *Explanations of the Ninety-five Theses* (1518), thesis 58, in: *LW* 31:213.
4. Luther, sermon on Luke 19:29-34, *Predigten des Jahres* 1523, in: *WA* 12,470.40f.
5. Luther, sermon on April 25, 1522, *Predigten des Jahres* 1522, in: *WA* 10 III,97.10ff.
6. Luther, *The Private Mass and the Consecration of Priests* (1533), in: *LW* 38:209.
7. *The Augsburg Confession*, article 14, in: *The Book of Concord*, ed. T. Tappert, 36.
8. Luther, *Infiltrating and Clandestine Preachers*, in: *LW* 40:387f.
9. Luther, in his exposition of Psalm 82:4, Den 82. *Psalm ausgelegt* (1530), in: *WA* 31 I,211.19f.31f.
10. Luther, *Against the Thirty-two Articles of the Louvain Theologists*, article 41, in: *LW* 34:357.
11. Luther, *Wider Hans Worst* (1541), in: *WA* 51,487.3ff.
12. *Lutheran Book of Worship*, hymn no. 28; and *Evangelisches Gesangbuch*, hymn no. 4.
13. *LBW*, no. 48; and *EG*, no. 15.
14. Luther, *Sendschreiben an Herzog Albrecht von Preußen* (1532), in: *WA* 30 III,552.14f.
15. Luther, *Lectures on Galatians* (1535), in: *LW* 26:66f.
16. Luther, *The Private Mass and the Consecration of Priests* (1533), in: *LW* 38:171.
17. Luther, *The Small Catechism, in: The Book of Concord*, ed. Tappert, 349.